ELDER ABUSE

Therapeutic Perspectives in Practice

Andrew Papadopoulos
& Jenny La Fontaine

Winslow Press Ltd
Telford Road, Bicester, Oxon OX6 0TS

First published in 2000

Winslow Press Ltd, Telford Road, Bicester, Oxon OX6 0TS

www.winslow-press.co.uk

002-2626/Printed in the United Kingdom/1010

British Library Cataloguing in Publication Data

Papadopoulos, Andrew
  Elder abuse : therapeutic perspectives in practice. – (Winslow editions)
  1. Aged – Abuse of   2. Aged – Psychology
  I. Title   II. La Fontaine, Jenny
  362.6

ISBN 0 86388 251 X

To Rita and Costas
Chris and John
Gemma
Alethea and Michael

with our love

About the Authors

Andrew Papadopoulos is a Consultant Clinical Psychologist. He currently heads the physical health speciality to older adults in South Birmingham Mental Health NHS Trust, and the Elderly Hospitals division of South Birmingham Community Health NHS Trust. He has worked primarily with older adults since qualifying and his work includes a publication on counselling carers. He is also an Honorary Tutor to the School of Psychology at the University of Birmingham.

Jenny La Fontaine is an Advanced Nurse Practitioner with Northern and South Birmingham Mental Health Trust, with a background in working with Older People in the field of Mental Health. Her career has encompassed both hospital and community work including being a Lecturer Practitioner. She also has an MA in Gerontology. She is currently facilitating a project in the early detection of mental health problems in older people within Primary Health Care Teams. She is also a visiting lecturer for the University of Central England.

Contents

Figures

Tables

Foreword

I AM VERY PLEASED to have this opportunity to express my enthusiasm for this excellent addition to the literature about elder mistreatment.

It has been commonplace in introducing books on this subject to remind readers that in the 1960s, we were shocked to learn that child abuse existed. In the 1970s, it was spouse abuse that became highlighted and by the 1980s, following the discoveries in the United States in the 1970s, we became aware of the existence of elder abuse and neglect in the UK. It has since emerged as an international phenomenon, eliciting similar responses from the service agencies.

During the 1990s in the UK, several important theoretical texts have been published which have helped us to understand this phenomenon, how to recognise the signs and symptoms of abuse and neglect and how to make responsible and sympathetic interventions. During this time, a number of books have been written by practitioners to inform and encourage other practitioners when they are faced with the reality of abuse in the practice of their daily work. In general, it may be said that while these practitioner books have been helpful, they have tended to lack a theoretical base from which to establish good practice. This book by Andrew Papadopoulos and Jenny La Fontaine is the exception to the rule. While the authors are both clinical psychologists with both practical and teaching experience, they have sought in this book to provide a theoretical ground plan from which the practitioner can inform his/her therapeutic role while engaged in field work. Such a psychodynamic approach to casework is to be welcomed.

After placing abuse in its social context, the authors go on to consider definitions of abuse and its extent. They do not ignore the legal implications and concentrate very helpfully on the psychological dimensions of abuse, including the occurrence of types of abuse in both domestic and institutional settings. They conclude by examining the implications for professional practice, placing this within the context of interagency and multidisciplinary teamwork, which they regard as being essential. They consider the nature of therapeutic intervention with both victims and perpetrators. They do not ignore the social construction of elder abuse nor the standards of good practice which need to be incorporated within a service culture.

This book deserves to be widely read and studied with the help of the exercises and suggested reading lists contained in each chapter and I wish it very well, hoping that at least one copy of it will be on each training department shelf as well as in personal libraries.

Frank Glendenning
Centre for Social Gerontology
Keele University

Acknowledgements

COLLECTIVELY, WE WOULD LIKE to thank a number of people. This includes our publisher, Winslow Press, including Graham Stokes, for their patience and encouragement. We would also like to give our special thanks to the many older people and their families who have inspired and challenged us in working with them.

We would also like to thank our families and friends for their patience, support, tolerance and encouragement, in particular Gemma, Alethea and Michael for their love and hugs; also to our colleagues at South Birmingham Psychology Service, North and South Birmingham Mental Health Trusts, Nicky Bradbury and South Birmingham Elderly Hospitals Division.

We also wish to remember and acknowledge Tom Kitwood, who has inspired us, and so many others, to believe that care, without harm, is possible.

Introduction

THE ABUSE AND MISTREATMENT of older people is gaining increasing recognition amongst professionals from a wide range of disciplines in the United Kingdom. In the 1970s various reports by key professionals, notably Baker and Burston, started to raise awareness of this issue. In the early 1980s, Mervyn Eastman's book *Old Age Abuse*, was published and became a landmark as the only book in the UK to specifically address this as a distinct issue. Despite this early acknowledgement, and a number of scandals, action has been slow. Child abuse and, to a lesser extent, spouse abuse have become significant social issues, overshadowing any concern expressed about elder abuse.

The abuse of any individual, irrespective of their age or status, is clearly an issue of concern. The abuse of older adults, particularly those whose ability and power to confront abuse is diminished because of compounding physical and mental health difficulties, requires special attention, for several reasons. Firstly, existing legislation in protecting the most vulnerable is both fraught with difficulties in its implementation and is often insufficient. Any future legislative plans will need to be tried and tested before this issue can be suitably addressed. Secondly, research has shown that older adults are unlikely to report abuse, particularly in situations where they are heavily dependent upon the person who perpetrates the abuse, where they are related to the person who perpetrates the abuse or where, owing to mental or physical incapacity, they are unable to communicate their circumstances to others. In such circumstances abuse is often chronic and hidden. Thirdly, abusive acts in themselves are likely to give rise to and further complicate other frailties in the older person. Finally, ageist beliefs are likely to influence the nature and range of services available for combating abuse (Phillipson, 1993b).

However, in recent years, major moves have occurred within the professions working with older people to raise awareness of elder abuse as a major social policy issue that requires action. With this has come an increase in the literature available and recognition of the need to train practitioners, both to raise their awareness and to enable them to work effectively with older people and their carers in all settings where abuse is identified.

Much of the current literature available in the UK has focused specifically on the need to raise awareness of the nature of elder abuse, and how it can be responded to at an organisational level. This issue is and will continue to be of considerable importance, but it leaves a gap, that of how practitioners can work directly with older people and their carers, irrespective of whether these are families or professional carers. This book has been written in an attempt to bridge that gap. It is designed for use by professional practitioners who work with older people. It reflects the authors' commitment to this important area and our belief that older people, their families and their carers have rights to high quality standards of care and support delivered by skilled and competent practitioners. It is designed as an interactive, open learning book, covering 15 core areas. Each chapter usually comprises an introduction, followed by information concerning the topic, case examples and exercises, and further information, ending with key points and suggested further reading.

It is intended that the reader work through the book in the order that it is presented to gain maximum benefit, but it is obviously possible to address specific chapters independently. The exercises or case studies presented in most chapters represent an opportunity for the reader to explore their own values and beliefs about elder abuse, and to draw upon their professional experience of situations where abuse has occurred. It is intended that they will enable the reader to integrate the information presented into their existing knowledge, but at the same time enabling them to challenge previously held assumptions.

It is suggested by the authors that the reader should have access to support or supervision while using the book, either with an individual who has some knowledge of elder abuse or by working through the book with a group of practitioners. It is likely that this book will raise issues that require discussion, both on a personal and a professional level. The use of a support/interest group would be particularly relevant in facilitating the synthesis of the information presented.

The book is divided into four parts. Part One focuses on enabling the reader to gain an understanding of the extent and nature of elder abuse. Consequently, it places elder abuse in context, exploring the experience of ageing in our society, the concept of ageism on a societal and individual level and the impact that this has on the lives of older people. The acceptability of elder abuse is then challenged. Definitions of abuse are addressed, followed by an exploration of the nature of abuse, the extent of the problem and the settings in which it occurs. Finally, in Chapter 3, the legal issues surrounding elder abuse are discussed.

Part Two focuses on the psychological dimensions of elder abuse. Initially, it explores the nature of relationships that older people engage in, and the significance of these relationships for their emotional well-being. Secondly, it identifies how this is relevant to working with older people who have experienced abuse. Signs and symptoms and the human experience of abuse are then discussed, and the impact of abuse on the older person, both in situations where the abuse has been chronic and long-term and where it follows a traumatic event, are explored. Chapter 6 considers the various factors that give rise to and maintain abusive behaviour. Finally, Chapter 7 reviews the various types of interventions that may be helpful in addressing such behaviour.

In Part Three, abuse within family settings and the different intervention approaches are discussed. This part begins with an exploration of the nature and structure of family relationships, and the impact of transitions such as the need for protracted care. Chapters 9 to 11 then explore in greater depth the therapeutic applications that can be utilised with individuals, with families and with others who perpetrate abuse. Chapter 10 specifically discusses working with individuals who have been abused, focusing on setting objectives and developing a therapeutic culture. The steps of abuse counselling are then described, highlighting such issues as advocacy, empowerment and the special problems that exist in offering such counselling.

Part Four explores the nature of abuse in institutional settings. The dynamics of professional caregiving are discussed, as are the types of abuse and the risk factors that are associated with them. Chapter 13 addresses abuse prevention, including a discussion of the current legislation surrounding the inspection of residential and nursing care units.

Finally, in Part Five, professional issues are discussed. In Chapter 14, abuse by professionals, professional dilemmas created by working with abused elders and support needs are explored. Chapter 15 argues the need for a comprehensive response to the problem of elder abuse. It summarises the main issues addressed in the book and emphasises the need for self-awareness in working with older people who experience abuse in all of the settings in which it occurs.

We sincerely hope that you find this book as stimulating and thought-provoking as it has been for us in developing it, and that it provides you with the motivation to go on working with older people, their families and their carers in situations where abuse occurs.

Part One

Foundations

CHAPTER 1

The Social Context of Elder Abuse

Introduction

The abuse of older people is the latest area of family violence to achieve some recognition as a serious issue in our society. However, it is also clear that this recognition is very recent. This is despite the fact that the abuse of older people was first raised as an area of concern some 25 years ago, in the mid-1970s.

'Granny battering' was highlighted in 1975 by Dr Baker in an article in *Modern Geriatrics*, which, while clearly identifying the existence of elder abuse, limited its recognition to abuse within families, specifically to older women and mainly to physical abuse (Eastman, 1984; Bennett & Kingston, 1993). Despite attempts to maintain the profile during the 1980s, elder abuse went largely unrecognised until 1988, when a major conference was held by the British Geriatrics Society (Bennett & Kingston, 1993). It appears that this conference was a landmark in spurring action to legitimise elder abuse and to educate the professions and public alike about its occurrence and the need for a response. However, it is clear that there is still some way to go before the abuse of older people achieves the degree of attention that child abuse has within society, stimulating the action needed from the government, the public and the professions. The response will continue to depend on how widely elder abuse is defined, accepted and understood.

It is therefore important to understand how the problem has emerged, why it took so long to be recognised and the implications of the way in which it has emerged. This chapter is particularly concerned with enabling the reader to develop an increased understanding of these issues. To achieve this, firstly, elder abuse is discussed within the wider context of ageing, considering older people's status within society. Secondly, the reasons why elder abuse has taken so long to arise and how it has emerged are discussed. Finally, the implications of its pattern of emergence are discussed, for older people, the professions and society.

> By chance upon that very day
> Roy's father's sister came to stay –
> A foul old hag of eighty-three,
> whose name it seems was Dorothy.
> (Dahl, 1983, p12)

This quotation from a popular author of children's literature demonstrates the common representation of older people, and particularly older women, in our society. Utilising terminology that is essentially about emphasising negative characteristics associated with ageing, it ignores the gains experienced as we age, and the positive attributes that are present in older people. From an early age, irrespective of any positive role models we might have, many of us are led to believe in various ways that ageing and old age are things to be feared.

Exercise 1.1
Aim: to enable the reader to explore their attitudes towards their own ageing and the characteristics they associate with it.

- Spend some time thinking about an older person you know and like. Think about words that you would use to describe this person and write them down.
- Read the following passages and analyse the way they portray older people.

> A horse, an ox and a dog, driven to great straits by the cold, sought shelter and protection from man. He received them kindly, lighted a fire and warmed them. He made the horse free of his oats, gave the ox abundance of hay and fed the dog with meat from his own

table. Grateful for these favours, they determined to repay him to the best of their abilities. They divided for this purpose the terms of his life between them, and each endowed one portion of it with the qualities which chiefly characterised himself. The horse chose his earliest years, and endowed them with his own attributes; hence every man is in his youth impetuous, headstrong and obstinate in maintaining his own opinion. The ox took under his patronage the next term of life, and therefore man in his middle age is fond of work, devoted to labour and resolute to amass wealth and to husband his resources. The end of life was reserved to the dog, wherefore an old man is often snappish, irritable, hard to please and selfish, tolerant only of his own household, but averse to strangers and to all who do not administer to his comfort or to his necessities. (Aesop's Fables, *The Man, The Horse, The Ox and the Dog*, 1949; cited in Cole & Winkler, 1994, p23).

Said the little boy, 'Sometimes I drop my spoon.' Said the little old man, 'I do that too.' The little boy whispered 'I wet my pants.' 'I do that too,' laughed the little old man. Said the little boy, 'I often cry.' The little old man nodded, 'So do I.' 'But worst of all,' said the boy, 'it seems grown-ups don't pay attention to me.' And he felt the warmth of a wrinkled old hand. 'I know what you mean,' said the little old man.
(Silverstein, *The Little Boy and the Old Man*, 1981; cited in Cole & Winkler, 1994, p136).

All the world's a stage and all the men and women merely players. They have their exits and their entrances; and one man in his time plays many parts, his acts being seven ages. As, first the infant, mewling and puking in the nurse's arms. And then the whining schoolboy, with his satchel and shining morning face, creeping like snail unwillingly to school. And then the lover, sighing like furnace, with a woeful ballad made to his mistress's eyebrow. Then the soldier, full of strange oaths, and bearded like the pard, jealous in honour, sudden and quick in quarrel, seeking the bubble reputation even in the cannon's mouth. And then the justice, in fair round belly with good capon lined, with eyes severe and beard of formal cut, full of wise saws and modern instances; and so he plays his part. The sixth age shifts into the lean and slipper'd pantaloon, with spectacles on nose and pouch on side, his youthful hose, well saved, a world too wide for his shrunk shank, and his big manly voice, turning again towards childish treble, pipes and whistles in his sound. Last scene of all, that ends this strange, eventful history, Is second childishness and mere oblivion, Sans teeth sans eyes, sans taste, sans everything. (Shakespeare, *As You Like It*, Act 2 Scene 7).

- Finally, think about your own ageing: identify how you would like to grow older and what your fears about ageing are.
- Compare and contrast these three areas, discussing your views with at least one other person, and note these down.

Discussion
It is likely that, in exploring your views about an older person you like, you will have used many positive words. This may have also been the case when you explored how you would like to grow older. In contrast, the passages portray very negative views of ageing, and these, as you may have found, are often reflected in our own fears about what may happen as we grow older. This gives rise to circumstances in which people deny their age as they grow older, and we hear statements such as 'I don't feel a day over 40' or 'She doesn't look her age'.

It is argued that these statements are based on a fear of growing old which is associated with a return to the dependency that existed while we were children (Itzin, 1986; Hockey & James, 1994; Biggs, 1993). In exploring the things you value about your life now, you may well find that these are the things you fear losing as you age: for example, autonomy, independence and choice. In spite of any positive role models we have, reaching old age brings with it an overwhelming fear of inevitable physical and mental decline, powerlessness and dependency. This stems from the way that older people are viewed, that is as a homogeneous group who have few meaningful experiences to look forward to or any positive attributes to offer society.

Ageism

It is exactly this view of older people, as powerless, dependent and requiring help and support, that needs to be recognised and that is related to abuse. The impact of this negative view is considerable. It fosters a situation where older people are perceived as non-contributing, as a drain on society and on their families. This is typified in the intergenerational conflict present in the United States, where the rise in the numbers of older people and their use of the health and welfare system are presented as the reason for the poverty of the young (Estes, 1979). It is suggested that this view is gradually seeping into the UK. Older people are discriminated against, purely because of their age, and viewed as less deserving than younger people (Bytheway, 1995). Their considerable contribution to society, both in their previous employment and in their present activities, such as caregiving and volunteer work, is ignored, as being of no value.

The term used to describe this discrimination is 'ageism'. Ageism is defined by Bytheway and Johnson (1990):

A set of beliefs originating in the biological variation between people and relating to the ageing process. It is in the actions of corporate bodies, what is said and done by their representatives and the resulting views that are held by ordinary ageing people, that ageism is made manifest. Ageism generates and reinforces a fear and denigration of the ageing process and stereotyping presumptions regarding competence and the need for protection. In particular, ageism legitimates the use of chronological age to mark out classes of people who are systematically denied resources and opportunities that others enjoy, and who suffer the consequences of such denigration, ranging from well-meaning patronage to unambiguous vilification. (p14)

This stereotyping is widespread and, as Biggs (1993) suggests, older people are placed in passive powerless roles where they have little or no opportunity to create choices for themselves that go beyond those which society, through social policy, has already created for them.

Many attempts have been made to justify the disempowerment of older people. Disengagement theory, first described by Cummings and Henry (1961, cited in Victor, 1987), is one such example. These authors suggest, following research on one specific group of older people, that active withdrawal from society and older people's roles within society such as employment are normal and desired by them, in preparation for their death. Apart from the obvious reason why this research is flawed – that it studies one group of older people from a particular community and then generalises its findings to the whole population – it also ignores the reality that older people are forced to disengage from society through such policies as that of retirement. Whilst many sociologists and gerontologists have rejected this theory, it is argued that this theory and others like it are utilised to deny older people access to services that younger people expect as their right.

An example of this denial is Callahans' book, *Setting Limits, Medical Goals in an Ageing Society* (1987). In this he suggests that older people should be actively denied medical treatment which would extend their lives, on the basis that they have lived their lives, that they have had the opportunity to make all their choices, and that the only role left for them is to step aside for the younger generation. It is suggested that he is advocating disengagement theory, and is justifying the refusal of active medical treatment on the grounds of chronological age irrespective of the quality of life of the individual.

The powerlessness and discrimination experienced by many older people has been described in more depth by authors such as Stevenson (1988), Bytheway (1995) and Biggs (1993). They suggest that the negative attitudes displayed by society arise in part out of a fear of our own mortality and the attributions concerning dependency and ill health that will inevitably precede it. Townsend (1986) and many authors since then have argued that the dependency of older people has been magnified by long term socio-economic policies to the extent that discrimination against older people is as ingrained as that against women and people from minority ethnic groups. This view has led to theories such as 'Structured Dependence and the Social Construction of Old Age' (Phillipson, 1993b) (see also Suggested Further Reading).

Exercise 1.2
Aim: To enable the reader to reflect on and develop greater awareness of discrimination that older people experience.

Below is a list of terms that are commonly used to describe racism, which can equally be applied to ageism, with a short definition of each. Spend some time identifying examples of each term from your experience and describe its impact on the older person.

Personal ageism: ageism that occurs at a personal level and can vary from psychological to physical abuse.
Institutional ageism: older people are denied their rights or receive less favourable treatment than younger people as a result of the policies and practices of organisations, (such as industrial employment practices) including social policies.
Discrimination: this can be described as any policy or practice which deprives a person of their rights because of their age.
Direct discrimination: this occurs when an individual treats an older person in a defamatory way because of their age.
Indirect discrimination: a written or unwritten policy which denies the older person access to services or support.

Discussion
In considering these aspects of ageism, you may well have found a number of examples of each from your experience. They will have clearly demonstrated how widespread ageism is, and how it is institutionalised within society and internalised by individuals, including older people themselves (Bytheway, 1995; Itzin, 1986). It is argued that the process of ageism is both abusive and harmful since the experience of invalidation, being given incorrect information (such as 'what do you expect at your age'), having information withheld and being subjected to threats facilitate increased disablement and reduce well-being in the older person.

Ageism and the Abuse of Older People
It is within this context of ageism that elder abuse needs to be considered. Through developing an understanding of the impact of

ageism, it can be recognised that abuse does not just occur within family settings, but occurs more widely within society. Ageism is one of the reasons why elder abuse has taken so long to emerge and be recognised as a social problem, and also, paradoxically, is now accountable for its emergence as a social policy issue (Leroux & Petrunik, 1990).

As Stevenson (1988) states: 'Old people come to be regarded as less than fully human and are therefore not treated as persons deserving equal respect' (p23). It is but one small step from this belief to either selectively ignore the abuse of older people, and therefore condone its occurrence, or to recognise it but take a narrow and 'victim blaming' approach, viewing the older person as deserving the abuse because of their difficult behaviour. This issue can be exemplified by the paternalistic attitudes of some professionals, politicians and individuals who are in positions of power and who, through their actions, devalue older people. They actively collude with actions designed to marginalise older people and deny them their rights to the standards of care that younger people demand for themselves.

This can be demonstrated in the numerous reports on care in institutions such as that of *Sans Everything, a Case to Answer* (Robb, 1967) and more recently the report on Nye Bevan Lodge (Southwark Social Services, 1987). These reports have clearly identified that elder abuse is prevalent within communal settings, yet to date there has been comparatively little research into this area, or indeed any significant evidence of willingness to commit resources to follow up the recommendations made by these reports. This is despite evidence which suggests that, for example, adequate training and staff support systems can prevent abuse (Phillipson, 1993a; Davies, 1993; Pillemer & Hudson, 1993).

The Emergence of Elder Abuse as a Social Problem

As has already been pointed out, ageism is considered to be one of the reasons why elder abuse has taken many more years than child abuse to be recognised as a social problem. In addition, it is believed that there are a number of other reasons why this is so.

Firstly, there is a myth, widely believed in our society, that families no longer care for their older generation, and that this situation has been worsening over the last few decades. As a consequence, much research has been carried out to disprove the myth and maintain the image of the family as a source of care and support (Steinmetz, 1988). It could therefore be argued that to recognise elder abuse as a form of family violence would undermine these efforts. However, this research is in fact, one of the reasons why it has now been recognised:

> A growing body of research has demonstrated that husband and wife, and parent-child relationships in later life can be severely strained. An especially compelling issue involves these situations in which the elderly suffer from direct maltreatment by family members or in which their needs are left unmet. (Wolf & Pillemer, 1989, p4)

The research has identified elder abuse as a form of family violence, but this implies that it can be compared with and responded to in a similar way to child abuse. It is argued that this is flawed both because older people are legally and actually autonomous human beings (Phillipson, 1993b, p81) and because the comparisons with child abuse reinforce the negative stereotypes of older people being dependent and therefore more vulnerable to abuse, a factor which has been refuted in research by Pillemer and Finkelhor (1989).

Secondly, demographic trends indicating a continuing rise in the numbers of older people have caused increasing alarm (Victor, 1991). This has led successive governments since the 1960s to advocate community care as the best option. Indeed, community care became a reality in 1990, with the entry of the NHS and Community Care Act into legislation. Many professionals and researchers have expressed a concern that the impact of this legislation will put families under increased pressure to care, irrespective of their wishes or, indeed, those of the older person. It is suggested that this could lead to an increase in the prevalence of elder abuse (Phillipson, 1993a).

The final reason for its emergence is that greater media attention has been paid to the older person as a victim of crime. Headlines such as 'Punish or we are all damned' (*Daily Mail*, 1992) on the rape of a 100-year-old woman have served to increase the fear experienced by older people, especially those who live alone. This is despite the research that indicates that older people are the least likely group to be victims of crime. Media interest has generated considerable activity from industry and the police in exploring how older people can maintain safety.

The Implications for Older People

Older people experience a considerable impact from these attitudes and the length of time that elder abuse has taken to emerge.

Exercise 1.3

Aim: to identify the implications of the issues previously raised for older people in relation to abuse.

Spend some time listing the implications for older people of ageism, the way in which the abuse of older people has emerged and the reasons why it has taken so long.

Implications:
- Older people's perceptions of their ability to reject abusive behaviour and complain about it are likely to be marginalised.
- Older people are unlikely to complain about abuse because of their concern that they may not be believed, it may increase the abusive behaviour or it may mean separation from loved ones.
- Owing to ageism, older people are perceived as incapable, and therefore choices would be taken away from them.

Key Points
1 Older people, as a result of ageism, may well perceive themselves as powerless and unable to change things and will therefore be less willing to complain about abuse. This is likely to be because they fear further recrimination, or that they will not be believed.
2 The need to recognise the existence of elder abuse remains an important goal, but the danger inherent in 'seeing abuse around every corner' could engender a response based upon crisis management, with all the inherent dangers that brings, including denying older people their rights to self-determination and choice (Phillipson, 1993a).

3   Any action in circumstances where abuse is suspected needs to be effectively planned and thought through, to minimise the risk of professional abuse.

4   Because of the way it has emerged, and because of the comparisons (albeit inappropriate) made between older people and children, there are dangers that any response formulated will use the child abuse framework. Older people should be empowered to choose, even if that means not being removed from the situation that is abusive (if they are competent to make that decision). Without this fundamental principle, we are in danger of losing sight of the reasons for raising the profile of elder abuse in the first place.

5   Whilst government has acknowledged the existence of elder abuse, and responded through the Department of Health and the Social Services Inspectorate in publishing guidance for social services and health on the development of policy guidelines, we cannot become complacent. There is still a vast amount of education required if the problem is to be given the response it deserves. The general public, and the professions, need not only to develop greater awareness of the abuse of older people, but also to recognise that abuse in families is but one facet of a much wider problem. Older people are subjected to abuse through the social policies and practice of society as a whole. Through the values held by society, older people are marginalised and disempowered, and until that is challenged, elder abuse will continue to be accepted and acceptable.

Suggested Further Reading

Biggs S, 1993, *Understanding Ageing, Images, Attitudes and Professional Practice,* Open University Press, Buckingham.

Bytheway B, 1995, *Ageism,* Open University Press, Buckingham.

Hockey J & James A, 1993, *Growing up and Growing Old, Ageing Dependency in the Life Course,* Sage, London.

Kingston P & Penhale B, 1994, 'Elder Abuse, Social Perspectives', in Kingston P & Penhale B (eds), *Family Violence and the Caring Professions,* Macmillan, London.

Victor C, 1994, *Old Age in Modern Society,* Open University Press, Buckingham.

CHAPTER **2**

The Nature and Extent
of Elder Abuse

Introduction

In the last chapter, the recognition that elder abuse has only just achieved the status of acceptance as a social problem was stated, as were the reasons why this might be the case. In addition to the issues previously identified, it is suggested by many authors that a further reason for the lack of response by the professionals is the lack of a clear understanding and definition of elder abuse (Bennett & Kingston, 1993; Kingston & Penhale, 1995).

Following the British Geriatrics Society conference in 1988 a greater interest in the nature and extent of elder abuse developed. However, this concern was limited to a few interested and motivated professionals who, in the main, carried out small-scale research studies, utilising many different definitions and, primarily, samples taken from professional caseloads (Bennett & Kingston, 1993; Glendenning, 1993). This was in direct contrast to the experience in the United States where, following the articles by Baker (1975) and others, professionals responded quickly. They are now some 10 to 15 years ahead of the United Kingdom in their understanding of the whole issue of the abuse of older people. Clearly, the research carried out in the USA and other countries, such as Canada, is of considerable importance, and we can learn much from it. However, to address this issue effectively, an in-depth and more extensive knowledge of the nature of abuse and the extent of its occurrence is required through research carried out in the UK.

Recently, detailed research has been carried out, contributing to our knowledge base. It is therefore the intention of this chapter to explore the nature and extent of elder abuse, utilising research and publications from the UK and other countries, to enable the reader to gain an in-depth knowledge. First of all, the chapter addresses definitions, exploring some of the early definitions of abuse and the problems of utilising these. Johnson's (1991) definition, which, it is suggested, is likely to be useful to practitioners, is then focused on. Secondly, the chapter explores what constitutes abuse, initially identifying the different types and exploring what is considered to be abuse within each of these categories. Thirdly, the research on the extent of the problem is discussed, identifying its prevalence within domestic, community and institutional settings. Finally, the chapter briefly explores the theories on why abuse occurs. (These theories will be explored in more detail in subsequent chapters.)

Defining Elder Abuse

It is clearly recognised that the attempts to define the abuse of older people have been fraught with problems and have engendered difficulties, in research, policy development and practice (Bennett & Kingston, 1993; Breckman & Adelman, 1988; McCreadie, 1996). There are numerous definitions, which have been utilised for many different purposes and which have themselves created barriers to a common understanding of elder abuse. Firstly, the inconsistent use of terminology has created circumstances in which agreement on what constitutes abuse has been difficult to achieve. Secondly, the terms 'abuse' and 'neglect' have been used interchangeably, again often causing confusion. This has resulted in a lack of validity in comparisons made in research which has already been published. Finally, it has engendered problems for practitioners in identifying abuse when it is occurring (Bennett, 1990a; McCreadie, 1991; 1996; Bennett & Kingston, 1993; Glendenning, 1997).

It can be argued that the problems in achieving a consensus definition have occurred for a number of reasons:

- The differing values, attitudes and beliefs of the individual or, indeed, any group of individuals who are defining abuse.

- The way in which abuse of older people has emerged has been primarily profession-led, with little acknowledgement of the need to consult older people themselves on what they might determine abusive behaviour to be.
- The lack of willingness to acknowledge abuse as a serious issue, by professions, the public and the government.
- The lack of discussion and co-operation amongst differing professional agencies which work with older people (Kingston & Penhale, 1995).

Exercise 2.1
Aim: to enable readers to explore their own beliefs on what constitutes elder abuse.

- Brainstorm as many words as you can that you associate with the term 'abuse'. Discuss these with a colleague, describing why you used these terms and comparing their views with your own.
- Discuss the following situations, defining whether you perceive them to be abusive;

Mr Johnson and his four-year-old son are walking along the pavement. They approach the kerb, getting ready to cross the road. Mr Johnson is looking for cars when suddenly his son lets go of his hand and runs across the road when a car is coming. Mr Johnson runs after his son and pulls him onto the pavement; the car has to do an emergency stop. Mr Johnson slaps his son hard and shouts at him.

Mrs Lowe has dementia and her husband is caring for her. She is very restless and will not sit down for a minute. The staff at the day centre do not know how Mr Lowe copes and they are concerned that Mrs Lowe is not eating very much. Mr Lowe was asked about this and he told them that he manages by tying his wife to the chair when she needs food.

Discussion

In the first part of this exercise, it is likely that you identified many different terms that signified your understanding of the meaning of the term 'abuse'. In discussion with your colleague, you are likely to have reached some agreement, but you may also have added words to your list which you had not identified before. What may also be significant is that, in exploring your understanding of this term, words you identified held personal meaning for you. Things that, on a personal level, you identify as abusive may not be so for another individual. This may seem obvious, but it is necessary to develop this awareness because it will influence how you define abuse, and furthermore the extent to which you would recognise it as occurring. In considering the second aspect of the exercise, you may well have formed specific views on whether these were abusive or not. In either case there are two issues that need to be considered: the act itself and the intent to harm. It could be argued in both of these situations that the act was abusive, but did the person perpetrating the act intend to cause harm? This highlights some of the difficulties present in attempting to define abuse. These issues are discussed further later on in this chapter.

Early work tended to limit definitions to physical abuse, directed at older women within family caregiving situations (Baker, 1975). This created a somewhat stereotypical view of elder abuse and it was not until the early 1980s that a clearer definition was proposed by Mervyn Eastman (1982), in the UK: 'The abuse, either physical, emotional or psychological, of the elderly by a caregiving relative on whom that elderly person in dependent'. He developed this definition further in his book in 1984: 'The physical, emotional and psychological abuse of an older person by a formal or informal carer. The abuse is repeated and is the violation of a person's human and civil rights by a person or persons who have power over the life of a dependent.'

However, this definition has a number of limitations. Firstly, it ignores other types of abuse, such as financial and sexual. Secondly, it assumes that, to be abusive, an act has to be repeated. What of the 'one off' attack by an unknown assailant? Thirdly, it assumes that those who abuse are always caring for the older person, which ignores two factors. (a) Research has shown that the person who experiences abuse is not always dependent on the perpetrator (Wolf & Pillemer, 1989); (b) the person who perpetrates the abuse may be the person who is dependent, as in circumstances in which the person has dementia and is aggressive towards their caregiver. (It is important to recognise that the act is separate from intent.) Fourthly, there is little attention within this definition given to the older person's view of what might or might not be considered an abusive act.

These criticisms can be levelled at many of the definitions that have been written although definitions based on this limited view are declining. Bennett and Kingston (1993) suggest that development of precise definitions 'would be a major step forward in order to provide a solid analytical knowledge base' (p11). However, they do argue that there may be an advantage to having different definitions for different purposes, in that different definitions could help to underpin procedures and processes relevant to achieving specific outcomes in different areas, such as protection and therapeutic growth, care management, research and legal action. Many authors have recommended the definition developed by Johnson (1991), in particular because of its facilitation of care management and therapeutic work.

In this definition Johnson warns against the use of the word 'abuse' to define abuse. As an alternative, it is suggested that the term 'elder mistreatment' should be used to incorporate abuse and neglect. This definition has four distinct stages, which are identified below.

Intrinsic Definition
'Self or other inflicted injury, unnecessary to the maintenance of the quality of life of the older person'. This stage of the definition is deliberately broad and focused on determining whether the older person has experienced pain and suffering, irrespective of when or where it has occurred, whether it was intentional and who perpetrated it.

Extrinsic Definition
'One or more behavioural manifestations, categorised as physical, psychological, sociological or legal circumstances'. Johnson suggests that this process of labelling facilitates the identification *process, enabling practitioners to determine the intervention strategies required.*

Extrinsic Definition

This explores the density (number and different types of abuse) and intensity (frequency and severity of abuse), thus enabling the individual worker to identify the intervention strategies required and, importantly, the urgency with which they are required.

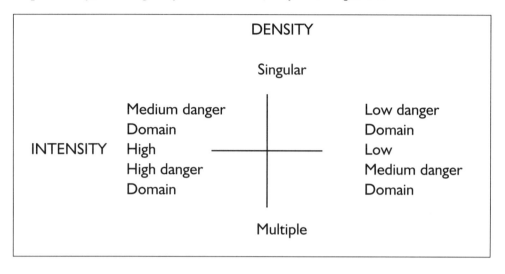

Causal Definition

This explores whether the mistreatment falls under one of four categories: active abuse, active neglect, passive abuse and passive neglect. The type of causation will determine how intervention is formulated on a continuum from passive measures, such as education, through to aggressive measures, such as legal action. Johnson (1991) argues that, to work effectively, definitions need to focus on the degree, that is, the experience of elder mistreatment and the problem, rather than on the parties involved.

This is further recognised when exploring the research into the experience of abuse for older people. Hudson (1994) in her research into the meaning of abuse to middle-aged and older adults identified a number of factors which emphasised the need to begin from the perspective of the older person:

• yelling or swearing at or slapping an older adult needs to occur only once in order to be called elder abuse;

- dependent and healthy elders experience abuse;
- abuse is inflicted both intentionally and unintentionally;
- the perpetrator's intent to harm, and knowledge of the effect or consequences, increase the rating of the seriousness of the behaviour;
- abuse determinations were made on the basis of both the action of the perpetrator and the effects of the action on the elder;
- the older people in the study valued early intervention from professionals.

Typologies of Abuse

Consistent with the second stage of Johnson's definition, there is a need for an in-depth understanding of the behavioural manifestations of elder abuse. Here again the literature has been somewhat confusing, offering multiple definitions and inconsistencies. Many of these definitions have been based on previous research, much of which has methodological problems and utilises anecdotal accounts from professionals. Pillemer (1993) warns against the use of research that is in the main invalid and unreliable to inform practice and policy. The following definitions are therefore ones that have been developed through research:

1 psychological abuse: the infliction of mental anguish;
2 physical abuse: the infliction of physical harm, injury, physical coercion and physical restraint;
3 material abuse: the illegal or improper exploitation and/or use of funds or resources;
4 active neglect: the refusal or failure to undertake a caregiving obligation, (including a conscious and intentional attempt to inflict physical or emotional distress on the elder);
5 passive neglect: refusal or failure to fulfil a caregiving obligation (excluding a conscious and intentional attempt to inflict physical or emotional distress on the elder). (Wolf & Pillemer, 1989)

In addition to the above, Holt (1993; cited in McCreadie, 1996) has argued that sexual abuse should not be subsumed into physical abuse, and should be viewed as a form of abuse in its own right.

With all of the above it is important to consider what is perceived by the older person to be abusive (Johnson, 1991) and needs to be distinguished from what might be deemed to be acceptable behaviour within the context of a relationship, such as shouting at each other. However, it must be acknowledged that there still remains a difficulty inherent within this, in that it may not always be possible to determine the severity and therefore the risks present if the older person is either reluctant or unable to speak about the situation.

The Extent of the Problem

Governments have argued that, to respond effectively to this issue, there needs to be a clear identification of the numbers of people affected by elder abuse. However, there are also those who argue that to continue to research the prevalence is futile. Stevenson (1988) suggests that a lack of a consensus definition, the estimates that are based on the reported cases of abuse and the hidden and taboo nature of abuse mean there is little point in researching the prevalence as we are unlikely to gain a true measure.

Perhaps of greater importance is the need to explore the factors that give rise to abuse and neglect, the nature of the problem, its effects on the older person and the person who perpetrates the abusive behaviour and, finally, the risk factors that act as determinants (Kingston & Penhale, 1995).

It has already been stated that the abuse of older people occurs within families, in institutional settings, and in community settings. There are a number of studies of prevalence which are relevant to these three areas. These are now reviewed.

Abuse within Families

In the USA, Pillemer and Finkelhor (1989) identified the need to carry out a large-scale, random sample survey to ascertain the amount and nature of maltreatment of older people. The survey was carried out in the Boston area, on a sample of 2,020 which was demographically similar to the population of Boston. They researched three aspects of abuse: (a) physical abuse (at least one act of physical violence against the respondent since they turned 65), (b) psychological abuse (the older person being insulted, sworn at, or threatened at least 10 or more times in the preceding year), and (c) neglect (the deprivation of some assistance that the elderly person needed for important activities of daily living on 10 or more occasions in the last year). The overall prevalence of elder abuse and neglect from this study was identified as 32 per thousand.

Physical violence appeared to be the most prevalent form of abuse and the findings were consistent with previous cases reported to adult protection agencies. What was also significant was that almost 60 per cent of the perpetrators were spouses, not, as is often believed, daughters and sons. The findings that more abusers are spouses has challenged many of the preconceived ideas about the characteristics of older people who experience abuse in family settings and about the people who perpetrate abuse. In particular, it supports the belief that elder abuse cannot be treated like child abuse, and has more in common with domestic violence.

The UK National Abuse Study

As has already been mentioned, research in the UK has been largely small-scale and based on anecdotal evidence from professionals (McCreadie, 1991). A number of interested professionals have recognised the need to carry out a larger scale survey in the UK, similar to that of the Boston study, because (a) we cannot apply the research from the USA to the UK on account of cultural variables, (b) there is a need to convince the government, the professions, the media and the public of the serious nature of the problem, and (c) there is a need to develop a sound knowledge base to facilitate effective intervention.

Ogg and Bennett carried out a survey in 1992, in co-operation with Fulcrum Productions and the Office of Population Censuses and Surveys (OPCS). This study explored the prevalence of financial, physical and verbal abuse, and involved 2,130 interviews. It established an estimated prevalence of; (a) financial abuse at 2 per cent, (b) verbal abuse at 5 per cent and (c) physical abuse at 2 per cent.

Methodological considerations (amongst other reasons) prompt these authors to point out the need to view these results cautiously. However, they clearly demonstrate the existence of elder abuse within the

UK. They also identify the need to carry out further research, focusing on the qualitative aspects of abuse and neglect such as causation factors, characteristics of persons who perpetrate abuse and those experiencing the abuse, and to explore other types of abuse such as sexual abuse.

Abuse in Institutional Settings

Whilst many reports in the UK have demonstrated the presence of abuse in long-term care settings (Robb, 1967; Townsend, 1962; Counsel and Care, 1992; Southwark Social Services, 1987; Lee Treweek, 1994), the focus of research in the UK has largely been on abuse in domestic settings. It is therefore necessary to review research carried out in the USA, to establish the prevalence. The problems inherent in applying US research have already been discussed, but the study by Pillemer & Moore (1989) highlights the need for research in the UK and justifies the concern about this aspect of elder abuse and neglect. The study sought to determine the prevalence of physical and psychological abuse committed by staff in nursing homes. The authors asked staff about abuse that they had observed within the last year, and abuse that they had committed themselves. The authors found that; (a) 36 per cent had witnessed at least one act of physical abuse, (b) 81 per cent had witnessed at least one act of psychological abuse, (c) 10 percent of staff admitted to committing at least one act of physical abuse and (d) 40 per cent admitted to committing at least one act of psychological abuse in the past year.

These results demonstrate significant levels of abuse. (This research is discussed in greater depth in Part Four). The results highlight the need for research in the UK, and as the authors state:

> The analysis presented here provides a preliminary picture of patient abuse in Nursing Homes. They [the figures] indicated that such abuse is sufficiently extensive to merit public concern. Substantial proportions of staff reported that abusive behaviours occur and that they happen more than once in the course of a year... Based on the evidence from this study... it may be a common part of institutional life. (Pillemer & Moore, 1989, p318)

Abuse by Outsiders

Whilst the vast majority of elder mistreatment occurs within informal caregiving, family or residential settings, there remains a proportion of older adults who experience abuse which is perpetrated by outsiders, often those residing within the older person's local community.

In such circumstances, abuse is perpetrated for personal gain or involves acts of hooliganism by people to whom the older person is not related or who see the individual as 'different', (that is, mad, eccentric or simply a nuisance, as perceived by that person). Yet, ironically, the level of social distaste elicited by such circumstances seems to have contributed little by way of researching the consequences for the older person.

Although the actual incidence of this type of abuse is somewhat less than expected by society given the publicity, the fear of crime amongst older adults poses a greater problem and can be a substantial influence in maintaining a diminished quality of life for many individuals. According to the British Crime Survey (1985) older adults are less at risk of experiencing all types of crime than younger adults. Taking street crime, for example, approximately 1.5 per cent of older adults are victims, as opposed to 6.9 per cent of people under 30 and 2.3 per cent from the ages of 30 to 60. Similarly, the younger to middle-aged group are 30 per cent more likely to have their homes burgled than their older counterparts. Given these statistics, one might ask why outsider crime against older people should receive prominence. The importance of addressing outsider crime is not so much related to the extent of the crime as to the impact that such crime can have upon individuals and the widespread fear of crime generated in this population.

According to Powell-Lawton (1981) and Conkley *et al* (1979), fear is associated with major health problems, both physical and psychological. Similarly, Cook *et al* (1978) suggest that, whilst older adults suffer no more injury or financial loss than younger people, the effects of these crimes are more severe. The following case example illustrates this issue.

Mrs Cohen was a 79-year-old widow living alone in rented accommodation. For several years she had been suffering from arthritic changes but, while experiencing a degree of pain, was able to walk independently and enjoyed a reasonably active social life. One evening, as she returned to her home, she was confronted by a burglar who verbally and physically assaulted her as he made his escape. Apart from assaulting Mrs Cohen, he had taken a substantial proportion of her savings, along with several items of jewellery and personal effects.

Her family doctor referred Mrs Cohen for psychological treatment approximately two months after the incident. She presented with generalised anxiety, sleeping difficulties, appetite disturbance, frequent nightmares and intrusive images of the burglar, and a fear of venturing out alone. Although over subsequent months of treatment she was able to recommence some of her former social activities, her health had somewhat deteriorated. In particular, she had had several falls during this period and took longer than usual to recover from bouts of colds and influenza. In addition, Mrs Cohen had planned a holiday abroad prior to the burglary, which now had to be forgone, as she was unable to finance it.

The above example highlights a number of reasons why older adults are more likely to experience fear of crime than younger individuals. Firstly, fear is often associated with personal capacity to deal with the consequences of a crime. Individuals who perceive themselves as lacking this propensity are more likely to feel vulnerable to crime and have a negative expectation of being able to deal with the consequences. As a result, such individuals are prone to developing a heightened state of awareness surrounding such issues, especially when exposed to stimuli which they perceive as threatening.

Secondly, the perception of threat is in itself likely to reflect an age bias, in that certain aspects of the local environment may hold threatening characteristics in the mind of an older adult, which may not be deemed to do so by a younger adult. Examples are graffiti on walls, noisy neighbours and gangs of youths congregating on street corners. Kennedy *et al* (1985) have shown that the degree of social isolation, type of housing and area of a city may contribute to high levels of fear in older people.

Finally, certain types of crime may have a more significant effect on the lives of older adults than on those of younger people. For example, the loss of one's weekly pension is likely to have a greater impact upon an older adult than the equivalent loss in financial terms for a younger person, who may be in a better position to compensate for their loss, for example by borrowing money from family and friends.

Theories of Causation

Many researchers have explored the potential risk factors of abuse, and five main theories of causation of abuse within families have been proposed. The risk factors specifically associated with abuse by family members and abuse in institutional settings are explored in Chapters 8 and 12, respectively. The causation factors of abuse in institutional settings are also explored in a later chapter. A commonly held belief, and one that has been discounted in American research, is that of the stressed carer. Eastman (1984), amongst others, promoted this view, suggesting that abuse occurred as a direct consequence of the unending demands of the caregiving role. It has since been recognised that the stress engendered by caring does not in itself constitute a major risk factor. Although many caregivers report significant levels, only a minority abuse their relatives. The question is, therefore, what causes abuse?

Exercise 2.2

Aim: to enable the reader to develop awareness of the factors that may give rise to abuse in families. After reading the following case example, highlight the causative factors for the abuse.

Mr Thompson is caring for his mother, with whom he lives. He has always lived at home. He has become more involved in caring for his mother in the last three years, since she was diagnosed as suffering from dementia. Their relationship has often been stormy and they frequently argue in front of others. Mrs Thompson refuses offers of help from statutory services. Mr Thompson has not been able to enjoy an active social life for the last year, which has resulted in the breakdown of a long-standing relationship. He frequently states that he feels lonely and trapped by his mother's needs. He also admits to having a bad temper. Mrs Thompson is isolated as a consequence of the loss of significant friends and her husband, and of her illness. Her need for company and intimacy leads to demands on her son that he is unable to fulfil and which subsequently lead to arguments. After a period in which she was experiencing early morning wakening, and wandering, she alleged that her son had hit her.

Having identified the factors within this case example, compare them with the following five identified theories of causation.

Intraindividual Dynamics

Abusive behaviour is linked to evidence of psychopathology in the person who perpetrates the abuse. Research by Pillemer (1986) highlighted significant levels of mental illness in the relatives of the abused older person. In addition, alcohol abuse by the relative was also found to be significant. Homer and Gilleard also replicated these results in a small-scale study in 1990.

Transgenerational Violence

While the theory has not been proved in research, it is suggested that abuse is more likely in circumstances where the person who perpetrates the abuse has been abused by the older person, or where violence has become the accepted norm within the history of that relationship. In these circumstances it is suggested that the person who perpetrates the abuse is either using violence as a learned strategy for coping with conflict, or is in some way seeking revenge for past abuse. Pillemer (1986) suggests that it is difficult to substantiate this, but that it needs further exploration.

Dependency

It has been highlighted in many areas of research that the physical dependency of the older person is not a risk factor. However, what has been consistently highlighted is the dependency of the person who perpetrates the abuse (Pillemer & Finkelhor, 1989). The person perpetrating the abuse is often dependent upon the older person for finances, or for housing. These researchers suggest that this situation creates feelings of powerlessness, with abuse arising as an attempt to regain control and influence (Breckman & Adelman, 1988).

External Stress
The presence of external stresses, such as financial problems, may act as mediators in leading to maltreatment. There is a need to consider these when assessing for the presence of abuse.

Isolation
Social isolation has been found to be present in circumstances where abuse occurs. The older person and the person who perpetrates the abuse may have little social contact and, even where this is present, the contacts may not be viewed as satisfactory. It appears that the presence of a supportive network does alleviate the risk of violence (Pillemer, 1986).

In considering the case example, you may well have found a number of these factors present, including external stresses and social isolation. What is significant is that the causative factors of abuse are both complex and interactive. Irrespective of whether the abuse occurs within a situation where caregiving is required, abuse almost always occurs within the context of a pre-existing relationship and therefore an understanding of the nature of relationships and their meaning for individuals is required.

Key Points
This chapter has emphasised that elder abuse is a significant problem in our society, and one that requires serious action. However, to achieve recognition and a response, the professions and public alike have to acknowledge the existence of the problem, as does the government. This requires a significant amount of further research and education. Current research and publications have begun to raise awareness of the nature and extent of elder abuse, but more is required to gain a clearer understanding and therefore a positive response.

1 Definitions need to be developed for different purposes: legal,

research and care management.

2 Definitions of abuse for care management need to begin with the rights of the older person and their perceptions on what constitutes an abusive act.

3 Further research in the UK is required to elicit more information on prevalence, reasons why abuse occurs, the nature of the problem, its effects on the older person and the person who perpetrates the abuse and, finally, the risk factors of abuse.

4 Although this requires further research, the prevalence of abuse in family settings is thought to be between 2 and 5 per cent of the older population.

5 The research from the USA suggests that abuse in families is more likely to be abuse perpetrated by a spouse. This requires validation in the UK, but indicates the need to move away from a response which is based on a child abuse framework.

6 While there are, to date, no studies on the prevalence of abuse within institutional settings in the UK, the existence of it cannot be denied and requires a response at all levels.

7 Although the prevalence of crimes perpetrated on older people by outsiders is low, the threat of and actual abuse by outsiders has a significant impact, psychologically, socially and physically, on older people. Responses by practitioners are therefore required.

Suggested Further Reading

Bennett G & Kingston P, 1993, *Elder Abuse, Concepts, Theories and Intervention*, Chapman & Hall, London.

Breckman R & Adelman R, 1988, *Helping Victims of Elder Mistreatment*, Sage, Thousand Oaks.

Glendenning F, 1997, 'What is elder abuse and neglect?', Decalmer P & Glendenning F (eds) *The Mistreatment of Elderly People*, 2nd edn, Sage, London.

McCreadie C, 1996, 'Elder Abuse: Update on Research', *Age Concern Institute of Gerontology,* Kings' College London.

CHAPTER 3

Legal Perspectives on Intervention

Introduction

Older people have a fundamental right, as do other adults, to the principles laid down in law of choice, self-determination, protection and freedom from abuse (in whatever form that takes). However, there is considerable evidence that the legal framework currently in place is either inconsistently implemented or not utilised at all. It is the intention of this chapter, first, to explore legislation, which outlines the rights of adults in law; secondly, legal perspectives on the experience of abuse in familial, residential and community settings are addressed, outlining the powers that are currently available; finally, the problems associated with the use of this framework are highlighted, with suggestions on how these can be addressed.

It is argued by Williams (1992) that the approach of the law towards older people, and particularly those where competence is questioned, is an example of ageist practice. He further suggests that the status of older people is reinforced by the low priority that is given to them in law, and that there is a need for practitioners to recognise the basic human rights of all older people. The UK is bound by the European Convention on human rights, which states:

> Everyone has the right to respect for his private and family life, his home and his correspondence. There shall be no interference by a public authority with the exercise of this right except according to the law. (European Convention on Human Rights, cited in Williams, 1992, p31).

This statement specifies that every individual, irrespective of age, has the right to make their own decisions. However, it also indicates that all individuals have the right to live without fear of interference. The only occasion where interference would be acceptable is where the older person would be deemed to be incapable of making an informed choice about their circumstances, in which case powers are available to respond to this. It is also clear from the legal perspective that comparisons of elder abuse with child abuse are inappropriately made. Unlike children, older people are not considered minors, incapable of making choices for themselves, nor do we have a statutory obligation to act for them unless they are incapacitated.

Honby (1982; cited in Collingridge, 1993) encapsulates the responsibilities of practitioners in the following points:

1   Where interests compete, the practitioner is charged with serving the adult client.
2   Where interests compete, adult clients are in charge of decision making until they delegate responsibility or a legal order grants responsibility to another.
3   Where interests compete, freedom is more important than safety.
4   Protection of adults should seek to achieve simultaneously, and in order of importance, freedom, safety, least disruption of life style and least restrictive care.

These, points along with suggestions by Collingridge (1993) which identify the ethical principle of a practitioner's duty to care, emphasise the right of the older person to maintain their independence and freedom of choice as far as possible, but also their right to have others act in their best interests, while utilising a course of action that is the least restrictive. It is with these principles in mind that we should explore the legal framework and its efficacy in responding to the needs of older people who have experienced abuse.

The extent to which elder abuse occurs has already been addressed. It is recognised that, although the figures of prevalence are an estimate, as Phillipson (1993b) states, one case of abuse is too many. However, consistent with the definition referred to in Chapter 2, there is a need to recognise that abuse and neglect occur on a continuum from severe to mild and, consequently, that interventions also occur on a continuum, of aggressive to passive. This in itself indicates that recourse to legal interventions needs to be assessed according to the specific circumstances of each case, and should neither be ignored completely nor applied wholesale irrespective of the wishes and desires of the older person and the severity of the abuse. Legal powers are available and should be utilised appropriately to provide an older person with the right to be free from abuse if they so wish. However, unless the older person is proved to be incompetent, we do not have the right to instigate legal proceedings without that person actively agreeing to this.

The issue of competence is therefore an important one. However, the current legislation is 'complex, fragmented and out of date' (Griffiths *et al*, 1993). There is no universal measurement of competence; it is something that is informed by various professionals on specific issues, such as finances through a solicitor or personal care needs through such legislation as the Mental Health Act 1983. A weakness of the current laws is certainly the ease with which a decision can be made about an older person's competence to make decisions, with that decision subsequently having major implications for all aspects of their life (ibid.). Once incompetence has been proved in one part of a person's life, there is a tendency to assume that they are also incompetent in all other aspects.

In addition, not only does the law inadequately protect older people, it does not clearly define responsibilities for practitioners once someone is considered to be incompetent, resulting in uncertainty about actions that can be taken on an individual's behalf.

At present there is very little guidance about the extent and limits of their [doctors, social workers and other carers] authority to take action or decisions on behalf of those unable to act for themselves... Professionals and other carers need to know the source of their authority, how far it extends, and where to go for guidance if they are in doubt. (Law Commission, 1991, p10).

Although, in practice, decisions about a person's competence may be based on the quality of the choices they make, in law this is not required. All that is required is that they appear to understand what is being asked of them (ibid.). Therefore, while the law has been reviewed with a view to making this process clearer, decisions on incapacity need to be made utilising current appropriate assessment and procedures. Before any decisions are made, the older person should be assessed to identify their capacity, using measures that rule out subjective judgements as far as is possible, and presenting information in a form that is most likely to be understood. This should include the involvement of appropriate members of the multidisciplinary team, including psychologists, solicitors, the police, doctors and independent advocates for the older person, so that decisions are taken in a way that protects the older person from further abuse.

The Current Legislation

Breckman and Adelman (1988) suggest that, following assessment, four client types be identified: the incompetent client, consenting or non-consenting, competent consenting client, the competent non-consenting client, and the emergency client, consenting or non-consenting. These categories will determine the nature of any legal intervention required, and the extent to which practitioners need to be involved in acting in that individual's best interests. The legal powers available at present are twofold: those pertaining to personal issues and those pertaining to financial and property affairs. The following section identifies the current legislation in relation to these areas. This will be followed by a review of their effectiveness in relation to the above categories.

Laws Relating to the Person

There are a number of legislative processes available which can be utilised to respond to abuse or neglect of the older person. These fall into three main categories: civil actions in tort which can result in injunctions or claims for damages, criminal law and certain provisions under the Mental Health Act 1983. Griffiths & Roberts (1995) suggest that civil proceedings are more likely to be successful than criminal ones, where the crime has to be proved beyond reasonable doubt. The capacity of the older person will obviously dictate the extent to which procedures can be used effectively. Griffiths (1993), outlines in detail the legal proceedings that can be utilised, and these are as follows:

Trespass to the Person
This consists of assault, battery or false imprisonment. Actions for *assault* can be brought if the person fears that harm is likely to occur, whereas for *battery*, there is a requirement that there *was* 'actual, direct and intentional application of force to the person' (Griffiths & Roberts, 1995). For battery to be proven, the intention to cause harm is not relevant, only whether the action was against the will of the individual. The authors suggest that the unauthorised cutting of someone's hair, or pushing someone in a way that is undignified and uncalled for could constitute battery. *False imprisonment* is physical restraint that is not authorised or agreed to. It does not require that the individual refuse, only that they do not give their consent. Consequently, this could apply to both relatives and professionals in care settings, particularly as physical abuse in residential care settings has often been found to be unauthorised restraint (Counsel and Care, 1992). Griffiths *et al* (1993) also suggest that it could include inappropriate use of authority to prevent an individual from leaving a room.

The Crown Prosecution Service can bring the action in these cases, or an individual can bring a private prosecution. In addition, it has been established that a third party (such as the police or a relative) can bring action on behalf of an individual. This could occur where the latter's medical condition is such that they are too physically frail to instigate proceedings, and where they are under the control of the person who committed the offence (Griffiths & Roberts, 1995). However, as already stated, civil proceedings may be more appropriate in respect of obtaining an injunction or damages.

Negligence
This can be utilised to prosecute a person who perpetrates abuse where harm is caused through either acts of omission or commission. It refers to instances where an older person does not receive the care and attention that they require, either through deliberate refusal or through

lack of knowledge. However, it is required that there is proof of duty to care, which could be proved for professional carers but would be difficult to prove with family members (Griffiths,1993). This is because there is no statutory duty for adult children to care for their parents, although the situation is less clear for spouses.

For a claim of negligence to be valid, not only does there have to be evidence of a duty to care but, in addition, it should be proved that there was a breach of that duty, and that harm was experienced. For professional carers, Griffiths & Roberts (1995) suggest that there may be a particular duty to care when working with confused clients. For example, if an individual who wanders has a problem with road safety and is not prevented from leaving the care setting, this could be argued to be a breach of that duty.

Wrongful Interference
Although the point is not fully developed, Williams (1992) argues that this action has much potential in relation to areas such as psychological abuse. An individual can be prosecuted if it can be demonstrated that the older person has suffered significant harm as a consequence of the actions of another, even if these actions were not intentional. Therefore, if an older person is subjected to psychological abuse, such as persistent threats to place someone in a home if they do not 'behave themselves', and experiences suffering as a consequence, the person perpetrating the abuse can be prosecuted.

For individuals whose capacity to consent to investigation and subsequent legal action is impaired, the legislation available is limited. Some provision for this is found within the Mental Health Act 1983, where various sections can be utilised.

Section 115
This section authorises an approved social worker (ASW) to enter and inspect premises (other than a hospital) in which a person who has a mental disorder is residing, if there is reason to believe that they are not in receipt of proper care. This does not allow entry by force, although it is an offence to obstruct the ASW from entering, nor does it allow the ASW to remove the person (McDonald & Taylor, 1993).

Section 135

This section allows an ASW to apply for a warrant to make entry by force where there is concern about the care of a person with a mental disorder. It also gives the ASW the power to remove that person if they are believed to be subject to maltreatment or abuse. The person can be detained for up to 72 hours but not treated. However, unless the older person fits the criteria for a further stay in hospital under the Mental Health Act, no further detention can be sanctioned (Law Commission, 1991).

Section 136

This section gives powers to a police officer, without a magistrates' order, to remove and detain persons who are considered mentally disordered and who are in a public place, for a period of 72 hours, on similar grounds to Sections 115 and 135 above; that is, they need removal either for their own protection or for the protection of others (McDonald & Taylor, 1993).

Section 7, Guardianship Order

This section gives powers over an individual living in the community to enable the provision of services which might otherwise be refused or to maintain an older person in residential care when they are refusing to stay. Its use is limited to the following:

1 to require the patient to live at a place specified by the guardian,
2 to require the patient to attend for medical treatment, education or training,
3 to require access to the patient to be given to any doctor, ASW or any other specified person.

It is necessary for the person to experience mental impairment to a degree that warrants guardianship, for that person's protection, or to protect others (McDonald & Taylor, 1993). Consider the following example.

Mr Cready, an 85-year-old man who has been diagnosed with dementia, is currently residing in a home. He was diagnosed two years ago and was admitted to the home on a Guardianship Order because of concerns about his safety and lack of insight into his needs and his difficulties in meeting these needs. Mr Cready has always been independent and self-reliant and, following his wife's premature death some 35 years ago, had managed on his own with support from his children. The reasons for considering guardianship necessary were as follows. First, Mr Cready demonstrated no insight into his difficulties or the risks that he incurred. Second, he continued to believe he could live at home, independently, but he had not been prepared to accept any help. It was believed that he was at risk in a number of different areas:

- He believed he could drive and refused to stop doing so. Occupational therapy assessment demonstrated difficulties in both construction and execution of normal tasks, implying that he could have great difficulty in driving safely.
- He was neglecting himself in relation to his diet and hygiene needs, and consistently refused help to meet those needs.
- He was wandering at night, going to neighbours and to the next road, where he used to live as a child.

Property and Financial Affairs

Financial abuse is considered to be the most common form of abuse and it certainly appears that, with the current legal situation, it is relatively easy to carry out. Many authors refer to case examples where an older person has been defrauded of considerable sums of money, possessions and property (Glendenning, 1993; Bennett & Kingston, 1993; Homer & Gilleard, 1990). However, much financial abuse can occur on a day-to-day basis, through the misuse of benefits such as retirement pensions, particularly with older persons who are incapacitated through dementia (Rowe *et al*, 1993; Langan & Means, 1994). There are various types of formal and informal procedures which are currently used to manage the affairs of someone where incapacity is considered to be a problem.

Agency
This is an informal arrangement in which the older person has the right to nominate an individual on a weekly basis to collect their pension for them, by signing the pension book, appointing that individual.

Appointeeship
Appointeeship is given by the Department of Social Security (DSS) to an individual, usually a close relative, so that they may collect the pension and other benefits for an older person where capacity is impaired. The DSS are entitled to visit the relative and the older person prior to granting this provision, however, there is limited monitoring of this by the DSS and, consequently, the opportunity for mismanagement is considerable.

Power of Attorney
'A Power of Attorney is a written document by which one person empowers another to represent him or her for certain purposes' (Williams, 1992, p35). This is a legal document in which a person is able to make it possible for someone to manage specific aspects of their affairs. It is required by law that, at the time of drawing up and signing the document, the person should be able to understand the nature of the agreement. It is also required that the person have an independent solicitor acting for them, rather than one solicitor acting for both themselves and the attorney. This will not survive the person becoming incapacitated; however, it does require the attorney to inform the relevant people that this has occurred. Again, this is not monitored.

Enduring Power of Attorney
This is instigated in the same way that Power of Attorney is, but, once incapacity occurs, it can survive by means of transferral to the Court of Protection. This therefore allows someone anticipating incapacity to make an Order for an individual to manage their affairs, giving general or specific instructions on how this should be done. Once incapacity has been reached, the attorney is required to inform the Court of Protection, who then act in a supervisory role. However, little monitoring takes place to ensure that an individual's wishes are being responded to (Williams, 1992; Langan & Means, 1994).

Court of Protection

This forms part of the Mental Health Act 1983 and is designed for the management of property and affairs of people who lack capacity to manage for themselves. The court has to be satisfied that incapacity is present, although the tests for this are vague and therefore open to subjectivity. Once it is considered that this is necessary, the court appoints a receiver who then manages the day-to-day affairs of the older person and is required to produce accounts and receipts of money spent on behalf of that person. The court itself manages the more significant aspects of someone's affairs, such as the buying and selling of property, and even the making of a will. However, the court has often been criticised for its 'all or nothing approach' and for the length of time involved in instigating procedures (Williams, 1992; Langan & Means, 1994).

In circumstances where financial abuse is suspected, recourse to criminal or civil proceedings is thought to be particularly appropriate (Griffiths *et al*, 1993). There are a range of procedures available, such as an action for damages where trespass to property has occurred, through to prosecution for theft or fraud. However, the use of such procedures would obviously depend on the circumstances surrounding the abuse.

Exercise 3.1

Aim: To enable the reader to explore the difficulties in utilising the current framework. The current legislation is clearly complex and there have been many criticisms of its efficacy in responding to the needs of older people who have experienced abuse. Read the following case studies and consider whether you would utilise any of the legal powers described above. Identify the problems that would emerge in either utilising these powers or not.

Case Study I

Mr Howard is currently residing in a nursing home. He has been told by his son and daughter that he is there for a short time only, and that he will be returning home in the near future. He has dementia, and, as a consequence, had been taking risks at home that were perceived to be unacceptable, including putting out lighted cigarettes on the arms of his sofa, which had resulted in a small fire. It is considered unlikely that he will return home. After a short time in this home, Mr Howard started to attempt to leave, insisting that he had to go home, and became aggressive when prevented from going out of the door.

One afternoon, his son arrives, to find Mr Howard in a distressed state. He has circular bruising around his wrists and is accusing a member of staff of tying him to his bed. The manager of the home reports that Mr Howard was very aggressive towards night staff when they tried to prevent him from leaving and that, as a consequence, they had to restrain him. This explanation is accepted. However, on the next occasion, Mr Howard has more bruising on his arms and is drowsy which makes him unsteady and in danger of falling. Again, Mr Howard's son is informed that the restraint and subsequent bruising has occurred as a consequence of his behaviour.

Case Study 2

Mrs Lane is a 68-year-old woman who lives with her husband and son. Her son has had schizophrenia for the last 20 years and has only lived away from home for short periods of time. Four years ago, her husband was diagnosed as having Parkinson's Disease and he is now very disabled as a consequence. To manage on a daily basis, Mrs Lane leaves her husband in the care of her son, so that she can get the shopping and deal with other essentials.

You have been visiting for a number of months to support Mrs Lane, and have managed to obtain a place at the day hospital for Mr Lane, one day a week, for treatment and respite. On his first visit, Mr Lane is given a full physical examination, during which it is noted that he has bruising around his thighs and buttocks and is also very withdrawn. After investigation it transpires that Mr Lane's son resorts to hitting his father with a strap when he is incontinent, but Mrs Lane was too frightened to report this as her son has threatened her with violence if she said anything. She has never actually witnessed this behaviour.

Discussion

In both of these case studies, the recourse to legal interventions could have been appropriate. However, they raise a number of important issues which highlight the criticisms of the current legislation and its application.

1   It is frequently argued that older people who experience abuse would be reluctant to prosecute. On the surface this may well be an issue in these case studies, in both of which those perpetrating the abuse are in positions of power over the older person. However, it is proposed by Griffiths *et al* (1993) that the same argument was used regarding domestic violence, but once the laws were made more 'user friendly' these problems disappeared. Inherent within this is the need for professionals to explore their attitudes towards elder abuse, and to consider legal interventions in terms of their viability.

2   It has been found that professionals often respond, even in quite serious cases of abuse, by ignoring the available legal powers (Griffiths *et al*, 1993). In some circumstances, the person perpetrating the abuse should be given clear information concerning the legal consequences of their behaviour. Professionals need to be prepared to consider legal courses of action as an obligation of their duty to care.

3   Various authors argue that the law does not adequately protect older people, in that many of the laws relating to the prevention of abuse are related to property and financial considerations (Williams, 1992). In those powers that are available, the older person's autonomy can be seriously undermined. Collingridge (1993) argues that it can be further undermined by some professionals who seem only to allow self-determination when the decisions made are in agreement with their views. This may be a problem in the second case study, where Mr and Mrs Lane may not wish to take legal action against their son, or may wish to do so if given adequate protection. This could be against the wishes of professionals who perceive their son as being mentally ill and therefore unable to account for his actions.

4   Elder abuse is not conceptualised as such in legal terms and, as a consequence, the people who instigate the laws may have little or no understanding of the issues of elder abuse and how to respond to it when it arises (Griffiths *et al*, 1993; McDonald, 1993). Although this awareness is changing, this remains an area of concern.

5   Clear guidance on responsibilities is often unavailable for professionals involved in such cases. In the first case study, the staff's duty to protect the client from harm, which may be necessary in that Mr Howard may be at risk of being involved in a road traffic accident, requires them to act in such a way as to prevent him going out. However, they could in these circumstances be accused of using excessive restraint either to prevent him leaving or when acting in self-defence. This example highlights how in some circumstances, staff working with older people face complex ethical decisions. Their duty of care requires them to protect, but to do so could also be perceived as abusive. (Collingridge, 1993).

Williams (1992) suggests that, although reforms are required for the above reasons, the law, as it currently stands, could be used more effectively to protect older people. Suggestions have been made which would require responses both at an individual, organisational and societal level in order to achieve this. (See 'Further Reading'.)

Exercise 3.2
Aim: to identify strategies to utilise legal procedure more effectively. Having explored the legislation, discuss possible strategies that you could utilise with the four client types outlined earlier in the chapter.

Incompetent client, consenting or non-consenting
In relation to the protection of individuals where capacity is an issue, a number of suggestions have been made. Bennett (1990b) believes that we could adopt a procedure called 'Competency Hearings', which is currently employed in the USA. This involves a number of professionals, including medical and legal representatives, assessing the person's ability to make decisions with reference to specific aspects

of their life. The function this serves is to protect the rights of the older people to make decisions in the areas where they are capable and provide access to independent representation where capacity is problematic. For older people in residential care, the Wagner report (1988) suggested that independent advocacy would be of benefit in empowering older residents. This has been implemented in some areas in both community and residential settings with good effect.

To prevent problems arising, when incapacity is likely to be a problem in the future, two actions are suggested. Firstly, living wills could be utilised, so that older people are empowered to give advance directives on their future care needs and financial circumstances (Williams, 1992). Secondly, Levine and Lawlor (1991) suggest that families should have legal advice on financial and property affairs as soon as possible after the diagnosis of an incapacitating illness. This advice should also be offered to the older person and may act to reduce some of the unintentional abuse of finances and property that occurs, as well as stating the legal position of the older person.

Competent consenting client
In addition to using the legal powers already described, Craig (1992; 1995) has suggested the use of elder mediation where elder abuse occurs. This process involves using a mediator whose role is to empower the client so that they are able to negotiate settlements in conflict situations.

Competent, non-consenting client
It is clear that, in circumstances where an individual is able to make a choice about intervention and chooses to refuse any help offered, those rights need to be respected. However, this does not necessarily mean that the practitioner needs to withdraw completely. The older person can still be offered advice and regular contact. Making information available to the client, in this situation, is of paramount importance and such information needs to include actions that can be taken. Finally, the practitioner could establish some form of regular contact point so that some monitoring can take place, with the agreement of the older person.

Emergency client, consenting or non-consenting
Not surprisingly, it has been found that arresting the person who perpetrates the abuse is a more effective form of intervention to prevent an escalation of violence than is conciliation (Pleck, 1987; cited in McDonald, 1993). This may be a more acceptable response than the more common one, which is to remove the older person experiencing the abuse (Wilson, 1990). McDonald (1993), amongst others, suggests that removal of the older person may have a more detrimental effect than the abuse experienced. Therefore recourse to powers to remove the older person needs to be seriously considered before being utilised.

The Future
In recognition of the problems experienced with the current legal powers, the Law Commission produced three consultation papers. These papers outline wide-ranging reforms aimed at three distinct areas: personal and financial decision-making (Paper 128), consent and medical treatment and research (Paper 129), and public law and the protection of vulnerable adults from abuse (Paper 130). It is recommended that the reader review them.

Key Points
Older people are legally entitled to the same rights as other age groups, which relate to freedom, safety, least disruption of life styles and least restrictive care.

1 Legal powers need to be used with sensitivity and understanding on an issue-by-issue basis.
2 The current legislative framework is inconsistently applied and offers little protection for older people and their carers.
3 Legal powers currently available fall into two main areas: laws relating to personal care and those relating to financial and property affairs.
4 Criminal and civil proceedings are rarely used, but have the capacity to be used in cases of elder abuse. However, such use would require a significant shift in the attitudes of the legal system

and professionals, and the proceedings would have to be made more 'user friendly' if it was to be effective.

5 The legal system has a duty to protect those who are incapable of making decisions for themselves. However, this system is often inadequate in responding to their needs.

6 Decisions about competence should be made on an issue-by-issue basis, using appropriate procedures and a multidisciplinary team approach.

7 Various responses such as advocacy can be utilised to make the current system more effective.

8 The law is under review for all vulnerable adults and this, it is hoped, will result in significant changes.

Suggested Further Reading

Griffiths A & Roberts G, 1995, *The Law and Elderly People*, Routledge, London.

Griffiths A, *et al*, 1993, 'Elder Abuse and the Law', Decalmer P & Glendenning F (eds) *The Mistreatment of Elderly People*, 2nd edn, Sage, London.

Law Commission, 1991, *Mentally Incapacitated Adults and Decision Making, An Overview*, Consultation Paper 119, HMSO, London.

Law Commission, 1993, *Mentally Incapacitated Adults and Decision Making: a New Jurisdiction*, Consultation Paper 128, HMSO, London.

Law Commission, 1993, *Mentally Incapacitated Adults and Decision-Making: Medical Treatment and Research*, Consultation Paper 129, HMSO, London.

Law Commission, 1993, *Mentally Incapacitated and Other Vulnerable Adults: Public Law Protection*, Consultation Paper 130, HMSO, London.

Part Two

Psychological Dimensions of Elder Abuse

•••

CHAPTER 4

The Meaning and Significance of Relationships in Later Life

•••

Introduction

The greatest percentage of elder abuse occurs within the context of a pre-existing relationship, either with family members, in intimate relationships or within the context of professional caregiving. It is clear that, as a consequence of this, working with elders who have been abused is neither simple nor straightforward.

In circumstances where the older person is abused by an unknown assailant, who perpetrates one attack, the recourse to the legal system is the most obvious solution (although, as discussed earlier, not necessarily easy to instigate). Where abuse occurs within the context of a relationship, in which such issues as emotional intimacy and/or duty to care are major factors, no simple solution exists. Much depends on the older person's perception of their circumstances and their willingness or ability to initiate any action. Indeed, it is possible that emotional involvement lessens older individuals' desire to make allegations concerning the presence of an abusive situation. To work effectively, there is a need to understand the nature of relationships and their meaning for older people. This facilitates an understanding of the older person's responses and assists in the formulation of appropriate interventions.

This chapter is therefore concerned with enabling the reader to explore the nature of the relationships that older people engage in, including their meaning and significance. The means by which relationships develop are explored, as are the factors affecting the development, maintenance and ending of relationships. Finally, the chapter will link these aspects together in an exploration of the types of relationships that older people engage in and discuss the significance of these in abusive circumstances.

Relationships in Later Life

It is suggested that relationships have central significance for individuals throughout the life course. Jerrome (1993) suggests: 'We need to exist in the thought and affection of another to be emotionally secure, well adjusted and have high morale' (p226). This is reinforced by other writers on the subject, who also argue that a basic need for human beings is to be social creatures and that relationships therefore play a significant role in fulfilling that basic need. It has been found that, without these relationships, we do not function as effectively. We are likely to experience depression and low self-esteem, to take less care of ourselves and to have a greater risk of physical and mental ill-health (Hannson and Carpenter, 1994). It has also been suggested that the importance of relationships to an individual increases as they age, as we have a tendency to reduce the numbers of people we are close to, and to invest more in the significant relationships that we have (Levenson *et al*, 1993). In addition, Jerrome (1993) has argued that being involved in a social network is the single most powerful predictor of survival.

Exercise 4.1
Aim: to enable the reader to explore the benefits of relationships for themselves and relate this to the older people that they work with.

Think about an intimate partner and a friend that you have. Under the following categories, list the *gains* you experience in being involved with those people: practical, psychological/emotional, health. In completing this exercise, you may have noted differences in the gains you experienced with an intimate partner and with a friend. These differences will be addressed later in this chapter. It is likely that you will have identified many positive effects which are equally applicable to older people. The following identifies the gains that are recognised in research, you may find some similarities with the list you created.

Practical

This aspect relates to the tangible benefits of a supportive relationship, mediated by instrumental exchanges, and is important across the life span. Instrumental exchanges involve the sharing of tasks, giving of money and practical help. They also include the giving of information, problem solving and helping to gain access to others who can be helpful (Hannson & Carpenter, 1994; Jerrome, 1993).

Psychological/Emotional

This area is probably the most significant in terms of the benefits of positive relationships, and is mediated by affectional changes. Indeed, it is argued that most of the gains we experience are related to psychological/emotional well being (Hannson & Carpenter, 1994). Weis (1974; cited in Hannson & Carpenter, 1994) suggests that there are six main areas where relationships are beneficial.

1   Attachment: that is the sense of emotional closeness and security that is engendered by feelings of belonging.
2   Social integration, involving mutual interests and activities which create a sense of belonging.
3   Reassurance of worth: that others value you as an individual.
4   Reliable alliance, where others are available to help when needed.
5   Guidance, information and advice are available when needed.
6   Opportunity for nurturance, being valued for what you do for your partner and being important for their sense of well being.

It is clear that these are areas no less relevant to older people, where, in the face of age-related losses, the presence of supportive relationships are crucial to adaptation and the experience of well being. As Hannson & Carpenter (1994) identify, the presence of supportive relationships can be a psychological anchor for an older person, having a preventative effect against the impact of losses experienced, such as bereavement and retirement. For example, Silverstein & Bengston (1991) have found that the presence of close relationships with children is an important factor in the survival of an older person when widowed.

In addition, it has been found that the maintenance of a strong sense of self-esteem is, to some extent, related to the way others view us (Coleman, 1993). In the face of the loss of other significant sources of self-esteem, such as work, relationships play an increasing part in maintaining a positive view of oneself.

Health

Bowlby (1980) suggests that the presence of meaningful attachments contributes to survival. Research has also shown that they contribute to both the prevention of, and recovery from, ill health (Duck, 1992). This has been found in particular with illnesses such as cancer, where a greater chance of survival was recorded, and heart disease. Given the increasing likelihood of the experience of acute, chronic and long-standing limiting illnesses in later life, this aspect of the positive benefits of relationships is particularly important, and has been found to be beneficial in a number of areas.

Firstly, it has been found that the presence of another individual to care about increases the chances of taking an adequate nutritional intake and caring for ourselves (Hannson & Carpenter, 1994). Secondly, Thomas *et al* (1985) suggest that older women who have good social interactions have better immune functioning than their isolated counterparts. Thirdly, it has been found that relationships with family and intimate partners are an important factor in the prevention of admission to institutional care (Victor, 1991). Finally, positive relationships are shown to be a powerful preventative factor in relation to mental health problems such as depression (Coleman, 1993).

From the above, it will be obvious that positive relationships are significant to older people. However, it would be inappropriate to assume that there are only gains to be experienced from relationships. Whilst it is argued that little research has explored the costs to individuals of engaging in relationships, it is inevitable that there will be some, but that the gains should outweigh the costs for the relationship to survive (Hannson & Carpenter, 1994). These authors suggest that there are three areas of cost: (a) instrumental demands: in that an individual is expected to spend time doing things for and with a partner, (b) emotional vulnerability: openness and intimacy can be rewarding but also may expose us to hurt and betrayal, even if unintentional, and (c) compromise: some life and personal goals will have to be sacrificed for the relationship.

It is argued that marital relationships are life protective for both partners (Jeffreys & Thane, 1989). However, it is also demonstrated that there is a gender difference, in that men gain more than women, as older men who are single have a lower life expectancy, whereas single women have a higher life expectancy. In this it can be seen that the costs to women of engaging in a marital relationship can be high.

However, it cannot be assumed from the above that older people are likely to leave a relationship that involves high costs. Victor (1991) argues that the divorce rates for older people are still relatively low. This is likely to be for a number of reasons. First, it is suggested that, given the central importance of relationships to our existence, the costs of leaving a relationship may well be higher than those of staying (Gross, 1992, Hannson & Carpenter, 1994). A second reason, which is related to the first, is that, in the current cohort of older people, the opportunity to leave a negative relationship is less, both because of the social stigma associated with such a move and, for women, because of financial dependence on their partners. Thirdly, the opportunities for finding further partners or friendships in later life reduce owing to death and ill-health. Finally, in marital relationships where partners experience primarily negative outcomes, it has been shown that they may redefine the negative experiences as they become more used to them (Levenson *et al*, 1993).

The Development and Maintenance of Relationships

> Considering what we may be letting ourselves in for, there might be a case for never getting into relationships at all. But we do all the same, because they provide so many rewards and create so much 'meaning' for us in life. The costs are readily discounted and we enter relationships in the hope of benefits. (Duck, 1992, p68)

This quotation emphasises the desire to have relationships that fulfil our need for meaning and hope in spite of the possible costs incurred. However, the way in which we enter into, develop and maintain relationships is influenced by the skills we have learned throughout the life course. Bowlby (1980) suggests that our ability to sustain relationships is based on our early experiences with parents or significant others and that our early experiences, followed by responses received from other significant relationships, will affect us throughout our life. The ability of our parents to facilitate a secure environment, in which we are able to explore and develop attachments with others, and to be worthy of help when difficulties arise, will influence our ability to develop and maintain secure bonds. In this theory, attachment behaviour is the means by which we achieve and maintain contact with another person, and is as essential to our development as is eating and having sexual relationships. This behaviour leads to the development of bonds with significant others, and to certain types of behaviour when that relationship is threatened.

The Types and Nature of Relationships

The relationships that older people engage in are much the same as at other stages in the life course, and each type has different meanings for the individual. Returning to Exercise 4.1, you will recall that you may have identified different gains from an intimate relationship than from a relationship with a friend. This acknowledges that certain types of relationships have different meanings. The next part of the chapter explores two main types of relationship that older people engage in, and their significance.

Intimate Relationships

Jerrome (1993) argues that intimate relationships are potentially the greatest source of affection and companionship in later life. Intimate partners are likely to live together, without other family members although they may prefer to live close by, for a significant period of time (Victor, 1987). Jerrome further states that intimate relationships in later life are characterised by the following salient points, which are relevant when considering the issue of elder abuse within an intimate relationship.

1   The quality of the relationship has significance for moral and life satisfaction, people who are happy with their relationship are happy with life in general.

2   The longer a relationship has been in existence, the more central it becomes to self-esteem and identity, and consequently the harder it becomes to disengage from it.

3   The way in which the transitions of later life are responded to, such as retirement or the need for care, depends on patterns of coping developed over many years and the degree of intimacy between partners.

4   It is a normative expectation in many cultures that older spouses will give care even in the context of a previously poor relationship. (Finch & Mason, 1990)

As stated earlier, the majority of elder abuse is considered to be spouse abuse (Pillemer & Finkelhor, 1989). On that basis the above points become issues which need to be considered when developing appropriate assessment and intervention strategies. The older person who experiences abuse within the context of a long term intimate relationship, irrespective of whether that is a marital relationship, gay partners or a co-habiting couple, has potentially much to lose by admitting that abuse is occurring. They may be concerned that the outcome will be the decision to separate them. For some older people, this may be a fate worse than the abuse, especially if the relationship has been established for many years and has become an integral part of their identity.

In addition, while the practitioner may perceive the situation as abusive, this may not be the perception of the client, and may well have been a coping strategy used within the relationship for many years, which is accepted even if not deemed appropriate.

Family Relationships
The nature and structure of family relationships is further explored in Chapter 8, however, it is necessary here to explore the importance of the family to older individuals. The family is often viewed solely in terms of the care that its members provide for their older generations but, while this is certainly an aspect of the significance of family relationships, it is by no means the only area of importance. The family is considered to be the place where most individuals have their needs for companionship

and intimacy met, through intimate partners such as spouses, as outlined above, or through children and siblings, (Jerrome, 1993). Indeed, it is widely acknowledged that society places considerable emphasis on the importance of remaining in social relationships: 'The couple and family orientation of social life and the value attached to sociability make the family or lack of it a main reference point in ageing' (ibid., p227).

However, it is clear that the quality of a relationship may vary considerably, depending on structural issues such as whether the family live close by, emotional issues such as patterns of intimacy within the family throughout the life course, and also cultural issues. Older people appear to view their families as increasingly important as they age, particularly after the loss of a partner (Jerrome, 1993). Despite their desire to live apart, many older people continue to have considerable contact with their family and this is likely to increase as the need for care arises. Qureshi & Walker (1989) suggest, however, that the quality of the relationship is more likely to be evaluated positively by older people than by their children. It is thought that this is because of reduced opportunities for establishing and maintaining other significant relationships and also, as Jerrome (1993) states, because older people may have invested more in the relationship and have more to lose if it fails.

In this context, some of the issues raised for intimate partners in relation to the experience of abuse are equally relevant to families, particularly adult children. The older person may well perceive the loss of the relationship as more damaging than the presence of abuse, especially as their social networks have declined, through bereavement or ill-health. Although the normative expectation to care is still present among adult children, the history of the relationship and the context in which that care could take place can cause considerable strain for both parties and lead to a breakdown in relationships.

Key Points
1   Relationships are of considerable importance to us throughout the life course, giving a sense of meaning and purpose to our existence.
2   Relationships involve benefits in three main areas: the practical, health and, most importantly, the psychological/emotional.

3   Relationships involve costs which may be offset by the gains experienced. However, even in negative relationships, the costs may be higher than those of staying.

4   The ability to develop and maintain relationships is a skill learned and developed over the life course.

5   Older people engage in both intimate and family relationships, both of which are of increasing importance in the face of age-related losses and their continuance may be a factor in the older person's refusal to admit to abuse, or to allow intervention where abuse is occurring.

Suggested Further Reading

Bowlby J, 1969, *Attachment and Loss: Attachment (Vol 1)* Basic Books, New York.

Duck S, 1992, *Human Relationships*, Sage, Thousand Oaks.

Hannson RO & Carpenter BN, 1994, *Relationships in Old Age, Coping with the Challenge of Transition,* Guildford Press, New York.

Qureshi H & Walker A,1989, *The Caring Relationship, Elderly People and their Families,* Macmillan, London.

CHAPTER 5

Signs, Symptoms and the Psychological Impact of Abuse

Introduction

The experience of being abused in whatever form and whether chronic or acute is essentially unique to each individual. Symptoms or features of abuse can be discerned in most people who have experienced abuse. However, the *impact* of abuse upon that individual is a product of; the nature and duration of abuse, the meaning and significance it holds, the inherent ability of that individual to defend against and withstand that abuse, and the social and material circumstances within which the abuse takes place.

For those individuals influenced by depreciated material and social environments and who may be experiencing poor mental and physical health, the impact of abuse is likely to be devastating. This is particularly the case for many older adults, who may also be dependent for their care upon the very people who are perpetrating the abuse. Understandably, older people may be reluctant to report abuse for fear of recrimination or isolation from their caregivers. In such cases, individuals are seen as particularly vulnerable since they often lack the power or opportunity to change their circumstances independently.

The present chapter seeks to highlight the experience of abuse and the factors which can influence its identification. Signs and symptoms of abuse are delineated, together with the impact of trauma and the long-term psychological effects protracted abuse can have upon the victim. As mentioned in the previous chapter, for some, being abused has become a way of life, often integral to long-standing relationships where the perceived boundaries of what is acceptable and unacceptable have become diffused. Very often, the causal relationships between abuse and poor physical and mental health are not recognised by the older person, with the effects of abuse being attributed to other factors which can mislead both the older person and professionals alike. In addition, changes to an individual's behaviour and physical health as a result of abuse can become superimposed upon their existing difficulties and illnesses and, as a result, are overlooked. The following case example illustrates this.

Mrs Green, who has experienced dementia for many years, was attending day-care provision for approximately two years. She had difficulty in developing social contact with other clients and had a tendency to fall commensurate with her poor mobility. Over a period of several weeks, staff observed severe bruising to her face; at the same time, she presented as very tearful and she had a tendency to call out repeatedly for her parents. When this was discussed at case conference, abuse by her partner was not seen as a possible factor since the staff believed the relationship between the couple was inherently sound. Rather, given that the client's home had an abundance of furniture, it was felt that she was most probably falling at home, as a further consequence of her poor mobility, and that her presentation was therefore a product of frequent trauma as a result of these falls. The conclusion was further vindicated when she was observed to fall several times within the day care environment. However, following several interviews with the client's partner, it became evident that, during this period, he was finding tolerating her behaviour particularly difficult. Although he never reported actively abusing his wife, his explanation of his caring actions strongly suggested an element of over-coersiveness in her management. Shortly following this period, the client was admitted to residential care, whereupon the bruising ceased to be evident.

A further complication to arise, which may add insult to injury for older people experiencing abuse, concerns the influence of an ageist culture. Ageist concepts can often influence both the extent to which we acknowledge the plight of sufferers and the way in which we respond to them. Comparison can be drawn between society's response to abused children and to abused older people. The knowledge that a child may be being abused will inevitably lead to a dramatic and well co-ordinated response. This is less likely to be the case for older adults at the present time. The lack of mandatory policies and procedures and of appropriate legislation for the protection of vulnerable older adults, and the lack of a comparative body of research in the field highlights this issue. Even where such policies and procedures exist, for example in the application of financial affairs, these are not always adhered to (Rowe *et al*, 1993). Furthermore, in areas of service provision which have applied themselves to supporting older people experiencing abuse, the services provided are often based upon unsubstantiated assumptions concerning the factors that maintain abuse and what should be provided to reduce the risk of its occurrence (Homer & Gilleard, 1990).

Signs and Symptoms of Abuse

Ascertaining features of abuse in older adults can be particularly difficult even for the trained and highly experienced professional. There are many physical, psychological and psychiatric conditions whose symptoms are analogous with those of abuse. Furthermore, whilst some forms of abuse may have observable physical and psychological features detectable in the individual, as in the case of physical abuse, other forms, such as psychological abuse, may not be so easily identifiable. In identifying features suggestive of abuse, Table 5.1 is intended as a general guide.

While the foregoing outlines the salient features of specific types of abuse, the clinical picture is unlikely, in reality, to be so easily recognised as such. Most forms of abuse are likely to have a significant psychological impact on the individual, in addition to the more direct features of any special type of abuse. As a consequence, abused individuals are likely to present with a complex picture of both physical and psychological features. This is especially the case with such individuals who have been subject to multiple forms of abuse, those who already may be experiencing poor physical and mental health and

Table 5.1 *Signs and Symptoms of Abuse*

Physical Abuse:	*Physical Neglect*
unexplained bruises, welts, burns, punctures, lacerations or abrasions (usually patterned or clustered, suggesting particular objects/implements/circumstances) unexplained fractures (principally to skull, nose, ear or facial structure) signs of hair pulling/loss evidence of past injuries (deformities of bone dislocation, pain/tenderness or swelling)	dehydration malnutrition/loss of weight hypothermia persistent hunger lack of appropriate aids constant fatigue/listlessness increasing confusion poor recovery from illness/ recurrent ill health
	Psychological Abuse/Psychological Impact of Abuse
Sexual Abuse recurrent genital infections pain/irritation in genital areas bruising or bleeding from genital areas difficulty in walking/sitting difficulty/reluctance with toileting/ examination.	difficulty with attention, concentration and memory sleep disturbance nightmares ritualistic/obsessional behaviour social withdrawal/aggression/timidity spontaneous tearfulness/ unexplained mood changes/fear depreciated self image/ suicidal ideation/self destructive behaviour appetite disturbances
Abuse of Medication adverse drug reactions affecting primarily cardiac, renal, hepatic functioning over-sedation/listlessness/falls hypothermia or hyperthermia confusion.	recurrent thoughts/images difficulty in communicating agitation/restlessness

Source: Adapted with permission from Declamer & Glendenning (1993)

in addition may be suffering from the effects of other stressful life events. The following case illustrates this issue.

Mr Hill was a 75-year-old living at home who, in addition to having severe osteoarthritis, was also diagnosed as having vascular dementia. Unfortunately, his wife, who was his primary carer, died. Following a case conference it was felt that Mr Hill would be placed at an unacceptable level of risk were he to remain at home and consequently he was admitted to residential care with the full support of his family.

On admission to the residential establishment, Mr Hill presented as being extremely agitated, and at times he was verbally abusive to both staff and other residents. He would continually question the absence of his wife, request access to his personal savings and displayed a strong desire to return home. In addition, his sleep was disturbed and at times he rejected his food. Initially, such features were attributed to his dementia and advice was sought as to how best to manage his behavioural difficulties.

Unbeknown to the services at the time, the couple's finances were being misappropriated by their children. Subsequent to the death of Mrs Hill, various events raised suspicion that the family were, in fact doing this. Following a second case conference, action was taken both to deal with the financial arrangements and to afford Mr Hill support and counselling with respect to his loss and the need for residential care.

This case illustrates the apparent ease with which abuse variables can be overlooked and simply attributed to the symptoms of a dementing condition.

Abuse and Trauma

Perhaps the most significant experience common to all abused individuals is psychological trauma, which, if left untreated or unsupported, can often give rise to serious long-term consequences. The effects of any major trauma upon a person, irrespective of its nature, has received much attention over the past years and reflects a common group of features, clinically termed as 'post-traumatic stress disorder'. According to Parkinson (1993), traumas have the effect of disturbing our normal assumptions about life, leading to confusion, disbelief, feelings of vulnerability, a loss of meaning and purpose to life and changes in self-image or self-esteem. In terms of specific symptoms of post-traumatic stress disorder, these include re-experiencing the event from memory on a regular basis, leading to emotional reactions, avoidance of similar situations or stimuli and increased arousal of the nervous system, often expressed by the person being touchy, jumpy or emotionally labile.

At an emotional level, individuals may often deny their feelings or express a sense of pointlessness to life. In addition, they may show apathy or inactivity, experience sleep disturbances or nightmares or become angry and bitter. At a behavioural level, people may show an inability to make decisions, display impulsive actions and have difficulty in concentrating. At a cognitive level, marked changes to an individual's attitudes and views concerning themselves, others and the future occur. Finally, they may become vulnerable to physical illnesses.

Parkinson goes on to suggest that people are less likely to cope with trauma if (a) the incident is perceived as particularly traumatic or life threatening, (b) the individual has poor coping strategies and inner resources, and (c) there is lack of support during the incident and shortly afterwards. Whilst the identification and prevalence of post-traumatic stress disorder in abused older adults has yet to be fully investigated, many case examples cited in the literature reflect some, if not all, of the features characteristic of the disorder. Moreover, the need for such research is paramount in assisting the development and implementation of appropriate assessment and treatment regimes.

Long-Term Effects of Chronic Abuse

Acts of abuse, like any other forms of behaviour are maintained by the reinforcing consequences or gain that such acts have for the person or persons perpetrating the abuse. This is not to suggest that abuse is always premeditated, malicious in its intent or even construed as being abusive by them, but rather that, where through the perpetration of abuse some form of gain is achieved (for example, in reinforcing power relationships within the family system to regain control over difficult circumstances), the behaviour is likely to occur again. Current research suggests that the majority of abuse perpetrated upon older adults is likely to be a function of previous difficult relationships the consequences of which hold particular gain for the person or persons perpetrating the abuse. In such circumstances abuse is likely to have been inflicted over a protracted period of time, giving rise to deleterious psychological, physical and social effects upon the person experiencing the abuse.

Regarding the long-term psychological effects of chronic abuse, this has been described by Yawney & Slover (1973) as the 'social breakdown syndrome', the primary features of which are:

- feelings of hopelessness or impotence in coping,
- depreciated self-image,
- loss of gratification with relationships,
- poor sense of continuity between the past, present and future,
- learned helplessness, leading to self-destructive behaviour (for example, obesity, alcoholism, social withdrawal and a disregard for one's own life).

Seligman (1975) developed the concept of learned helplessness as a model for understanding reactive depression (that is, depression caused by external rather than internal events). He described what happens to an individual when prior exposure to uncontrollable aversive experiences interferes with the natural tendency to escape or avoid such experiences. Briefly, the model suggests that in normal circumstances an individual, when exposed to a threatening or traumatic experience, learns that successful confrontation or avoidance leads to relief. The relief acts as a 'reinforcer' or gain, which increases the probability of that individual responding in a similar way under similar circumstances. Learning to respond in this way takes place not only at a behavioural level but at a cognitive level, in that the individual develops a belief in their own capacity to be successful in dealing with such circumstances.

However, in circumstances where the trauma cannot be controlled, that is where repeated attempts to deal with aversive experiences do not lead to relief, three primary effects occur. First is a *motivational effect*. Ordinarily, the incentive for making a response underlines the expectation of relief. If, however, the individual has learned that their responses have little or no effect in preventing the trauma, then this leads to passivity. Second is a *cognitive effect*. Following repeated failures to gain relief, the individual will often develop a belief that, whatever they do to try and cope with the situation, it will not affect their circumstances. This is likely to then affect their self-confidence and severely undermine their self-esteem. Furthermore, if this individual is led to believe that they are ultimately the cause of such trauma, this is likely to give rise to a more protracted view of themselves as being essentially a 'bad' person, which can elicit feelings of guilt and self reproach. Finally, there is an *emotional effect*. Shock gives rise to conditioned fear when it occurs in the presence of the threatening situation. Not only does such fear, if prolonged, raise the risk of psychosomatic illnesses occurring, but the individual can also become sensitised to similar situations where they are then likely to experience generalised anxiety.

The extent to which an individual, experiencing learned helplessness, is likely to engage in self-destructive behaviour is understandable. If attempts to deal with or avoid successive traumas are unsuccessful, leading to prolonged fear, it is likely that they will turn inward in an attempt to suppress or neutralise the intense feelings they experience, especially if their sense of self-worth is minimal.

Exercise 5.1

General Hospital

An 85-year-old female is admitted to your ward of a general hospital for rehabilitation following a fractured neck of femur. After initial progress over the first week, you notice that she has started to avoid her treatment, preferring to remain in bed. The night staff report that her sleep is disturbed and that she has been observed to call out in her sleep. Further, when she is visited by her partner, she becomes withdrawn and uncommunicative. When assisting the patient with bathing, you notice strange bruising to her back.

Having discussed this with your colleagues, a number of them suggest that the bruising is probably due to occasional falls against furniture, and the fact that she has been in hospital for some time probably accounts for her anxiety and withdrawal. You, however, are not convinced. You suspect possible abuse. In the light of the current circumstances, what other physical and psychological features to support your concerns would you be looking for?

Exercise 5.2

Home Visit

You visit at home, on a regular basis, a 75-year-old male who is known to experience dementia. He is currently living with his daughter and son-in-law, who are themselves in extreme financial difficulty due to recent job redundancy.

Over the past three visits you have noticed that your client looks pale and emaciated, and has become more confused than usual. Further, your client's daughter and son-in-law have declined to spend time with you as on previous visits and have become somewhat reluctant to discuss the current deterioration in their father's health. You suspect possible neglect. What further features and information would you seek in support of your concerns?

Exercise 5.3

Day Centre

You are the keyworker for a 73-year-old woman who lives alone and attends your day centre for social care. While she is physically frail, she enjoys the contact with other clients and takes part in most of the activities available. She lost her husband last year. You have recently been informed that about three weeks ago her house was broken into and she was verbally threatened by the intruders, who also stole her savings and various items of jewellery. On her last visit, you noticed that she had become withdrawn and reported difficulty in eating her food. There may be several reasons for this presentation, but you suspect that she may be suffering from post-traumatic stress disorder. You decide to investigate further. During your discussion with your client, what information or features would you wish to elucidate in support of your suspicions?

Exercise 5.4

Long Stay Environment

You have recently been employed as a care worker in a residential establishment for older adults. One of the clients you work with is a rather obese gentleman who tends to keep himself to himself. He shows very little inclination to take part in either recreational or social activities and you understand from his case file that he was treated for alcohol addiction in the past. What further information from this client's case history and current behaviour would you look for which might lead you to believe that he has experienced prolonged abuse in the past?

Key Points

1 While various signs and symptoms can be associated with specific types of abuse, the experience of being abused is unique to the individual and is a product of:
   - the nature, duration and frequency of abusive experiences,
   - the availability of appropriate support,
   - the inherent ability of the individual to cope with the abuse,
   - their existing level of physical and mental health,
   - the meaning their experiences have for them,
   - the compound effects of associated stressful events and the wider effects of an ageist culture.

2 Abusive experiences, irrespective of their nature, are often traumatic and can give rise to severe stress reactions, commonly described as 'post-traumatic stress disorder'.

3 Such stress reactions, especially if prolonged, can have serious physical and psychological consequences for the victim, described as the 'social breakdown syndrome', which often leads to self-destructive behaviour.

Suggested Further Reading

Eastman M, 1994, *Old Age Abuse – A New Perspective*, 2nd edn, Chapman & Hall, Age Concern.

Parkinson F, 1993, *Post-Trauma Stress*, Shedton Press, London.

Tedeschi RG & Calhoun LG, 1995, *Trauma and Transformation – Growing in the Aftermath of Suffering*, Sage, Thousand Oaks

CHAPTER 6

Understanding Abusive Behaviour

Introduction

There have been many theories postulated to explain why abuse occurs. Some theories highlight the relevance of social and economic factors, whilst others focus upon moral or biological issues. Clearly, the whole field of explanation is a complex one and is likely to remain so for many years to come. The essence of the present chapter, while not negating any of the above, is focused primarily upon the psychological domain as this has direct relevance to therapeutic issues rather than to wider social, economic or political policy.

Therapeutic interventions necessitate having a clear understanding of those psychological processes which underpin abuse. As Sidell (1995) points out, 'how we see influences how we know which influences how we do'. Within a psychological framework, abuse is 'seen' as a product of ways of thinking, ways of feeling and ways of behaving in the context of one's social and material environment. 'Knowing' reflects our understanding of these factors and how they operate together in the context of a relationship or set of social circumstances. 'Doing' is the way in which we intervene, based upon our knowledge or working model of this relationship.

Simply stated, the psychological approach seeks to identify and understand those factors which give rise to and maintain abuse behaviour in order to help individuals and their families to continue with their lives without recourse to abusive acts. Therefore, in order to understand abusive behaviour within a psychological context, this chapter offers an initial summary regarding the basic principles which govern our behaviour, and then goes on to offer several explanations or reasons why abuse occurs, based upon these principles.

Fundamentals of Behaviour

All forms of social behaviour, whether simple or complex, are underpinned by a number of basic principles which are identified below.

Behaviour is Purposeful

Social behaviour does not occur haphazardly or in isolation from an individual's environment. Rather, behaviour is learned and it serves a function specific to that individual. It may be directed towards meeting one's underlying needs (physical, social or psychological), as a means of communication, or more generally as a way of adapting to one's physical or social environment. This does not imply, however, that behaviour is always premeditated. There are many occasions where behaviour occurs spontaneously in response to some internal or external event or 'trigger'. For example, we may laugh in response to a joke or cry in response to a painful experience. Whether a behaviour is chosen or occurs spontaneously, our behaviour enables us to adapt to life's challenges and to draw meaning from our experiences.

The Outcome of the Behaviour Influences its Future Occurrence

When we behave in a particular way, there is usually some form of consequence or 'gain' that we experience as a result. Where there continues to be a gain in response to our behaviour, the likelihood is that we will behave in similar ways again under similar circumstances. Conversely, if the consequence of our behaviour either does not illicit gain or gives rise to a deleterious experience, it is unlikely that we will produce that behaviour again.

The concept of psychological gain as a primary influence on our behaviour is extremely important. It reflects the basis of the way we direct both our lives and our relationships. Briefly stated, we do not do anything in life unless there is some form of gain to us. Clearly, there are many circumstances where one might ask oneself, 'What on earth could I be getting out of this situation?' The answer is that there is some benefit to be gained from it, even though it may not be obvious on initial exploration. The reason for this, and what forms the basis of understanding abuse behaviour, is that the gain is not always a positive experience. Rather, gain can take the form of preventing an individual from experiencing a threatening or distressing event. For example, while being in employment may offer many positive gains, such as job satisfaction, money and a sense of purpose, not being in employment could put at risk one's family, relationships, the family home and so on. In circumstances where the job may not provide much in the way of positive gain, the fact that not having it would be disastrous is sufficient in terms of gain for one to continue in that job. In this way, gain can be positive or negative. Either way, the behaviour continues to be sustained.

A final point to recognise is that gain is unique to any individual. The value we place upon any consequence to our behaviour is a matter of individual preference and influenced by our needs at the time and what we believe is important and necessary for us, both now and in the future. Consequently, the value we hold for a given gain can change as our circumstances change and as we develop as individuals throughout our lives.

Behaviour is Motivationally Driven
Inasmuch as behaviour is a function of the gain it achieves, our behaviour is motivated towards achieving that gain. Under normal circumstances, our motivation to achieve a particular objective reflects the importance we attribute to that objective and is often mediated by our emotional state at the time. In this way, motivation reflects both our values and feelings surrounding a particular situation.

Where an individual's motivation to achieve a certain gain is high, they will often continue to behave in a particular way even if the gain they seek is not always immediately apparent. A powerful example of this effect can be seen in accounts of prisoners of war during the Second World War, where the motivation to escape continued to be strong even when they experienced successive failures. For some, the importance of being able to disclose to the world the crimes against humanity that were being experienced was a sufficient motivator to sustain repeated attempts at escaping. For others, the discomfort and distress experienced during captivity had a similar effect.

According to Maslow (1954) our needs play an important role in motivation. He suggests that we have a hierarchy of needs, from our basic physical needs to those which reflect a sense of spiritual comfort and well-being. He goes on to suggest that we are motivationally driven to meet each successive level of need only when the previous one has been met. Table 6.1 illustrates this relationship.

There are circumstances, however, where one's motivation can be diminished in spite of the need to meet one's objectives. Such circumstances usually comprise a state of physical ill-health or exhaustion, depression, drug intoxication, brain damage and other such conditions.

Table 6.1 *Maslow's Hierarchy of Needs*

Need	Description
Self-actualisation	Self-fulfilment in one's relationships. Increased self acceptance, acceptance of others. Autonomy and realisation of one's potential. Increased resistance to enculturation.
Aesthetic	Symmetry, order and beauty. Spiritual fulfilment.
Cognitive	To understand/draw meaning from experiences. To explore and to know.
Esteem	To achieve/become successful/competent. To gain approval, value and acceptance.
Belongingness	To affiliate with others. To gain emotional nurturing and a sense of belonging.
Safety	To feel secure, safe and out of danger.
Physiological	To meet hunger, thirst and so on.

Note: Needs that are low in the hierarchy must be at least partially satisfied before those that are higher can become important sources of motivation.
Source: Adapted from Maslow (1954).

We can summarise the basic rules of behaviour in the following way:

1   We behave in particular ways in order to achieve certain outcomes or gains.
2   Such gains are desired, in that we see them as important and necessary in order to meet our various physical, social and psychological needs and/or those of others.
3   The extent to which such gains are important to us reflects the level and nature of motivation in attempting to achieve them.
4   Whether or not such gains are achieved will influence our propensity for behaving in similar ways again under similar circumstances.

Exercise 6.1
Aim: To enable the reader to understand the purpose of engaging in particular behaviours.

Try and identify three major aspects to your life or three major experiences that you are currently involved with such as your work, an intimate relationship or hobby. First, on the basis of Maslow's hierarchy, try and identify the needs that each area is serving for you. Secondly identify the specific gains such aspects hold for you as reflecting your identified needs and which keep you involved in those experiences. Note that some gains may be positive, in that they are directly rewarding, while others may be negative, in that they may be preventing you experiencing some form of threat.

On balance, you will probably conclude that each experience serves to meet several needs and affords a combination of both positive and negative gains.

Applying the Principles to Understanding Abusive Behaviour
The main issue highlighted in the previous section is that behaviour serves a function, irrespective of the nature of that behaviour. The function it serves reflects the nature of gain experienced by an individual as a result of their behaviour. In order to understand abusive behaviour, it is important that we are able to ascertain precisely what function that behaviour serves for the individual or individuals perpetrating it.

When exploring the literature on abuse, it is evident that there has been much research focused upon ascertaining personal characteristics of the perpetrators. This may, arguably, be helpful in identifying potential abusers, but it does little to promote our understanding of abuse behaviour within specific contexts and can often lead to the inappropriate stereotyping of individuals.

What is required in assessing the risk of abuse is not what constitutes at risk individuals but what constitutes at risk behaviour. We therefore need to be addressing, not what are the characteristics of individuals but rather (a) in what situations does the abuse occur? and (b) what is the function served by the behaviour for the individual or individuals perpetrating the abuse, that is, what they are gaining from it, and why? It will then be possible to ask a third question: what needs to change, and how, in order to reduce the risk of that behaviour occurring again. The first two are the basis of any abuse assessment whilst the third is the basis for intervention planning.

In attempting to understand abusive behaviour in this way, a number of explanations or models are described which reflect the different functions such behaviour can serve within various contexts (see Figure 6.1).

Abuse as a Way of Establishing Social Control
Relationships continually undergo changes, partly as a product of people's development and partly as a response to major events. Indeed, while change is both important and necessary, adapting to change may not be in everyone's interest, particularly if those changes are likely to involve major losses for individuals or to lead to major changes in their life style. The effort invested in making those changes by those to whom the changes are important is often matched by an opposing effort by those who object or who are unprepared to make the changes.

In such circumstances major conflicts are likely to ensue where abuse can serve a controlling or mediating function. This is particularly evident where the expression of an abusive act is construed as a normal or acceptable way of operating under such circumstances. The following example illustrates this issue.

Figure 6.1 *Primary functions that abusive behaviour serves*

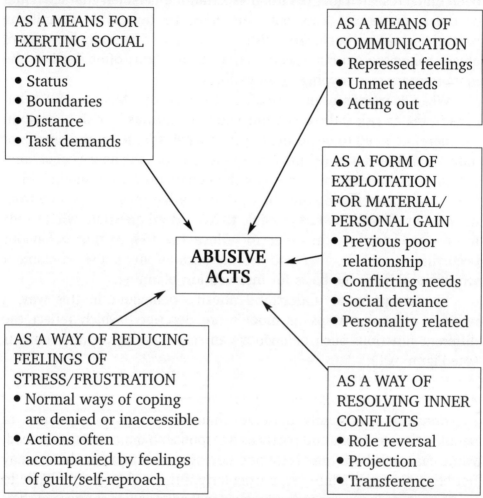

AS A MEANS FOR
EXERTING SOCIAL
CONTROL
- Status
- Boundaries
- Distance
- Task demands

AS A MEANS OF
COMMUNICATION
- Repressed feelings
- Unmet needs
- Acting out

AS A FORM OF
EXPLOITATION
FOR MATERIAL/
PERSONAL GAIN
- Previous poor
  relationship
- Conflicting needs
- Social deviance
- Personality related

ABUSIVE ACTS

AS A WAY OF REDUCING
FEELINGS OF
STRESS/FRUSTRATION
- Normal ways of coping
  are denied or inaccessible
- Actions often
  accompanied by feelings
  of guilt/self-reproach

AS A WAY OF
RESOLVING INNER
CONFLICTS
- Role reversal
- Projection
- Transference

William is a 75-year-old who suffers from Parkinson's Disease and mild confusion. He is cared for at home by his wife, Mary. Throughout their relationship William has adopted the more dominant role, inflicting, on occasions physical abuse on Mary as a means of controlling her behaviour. Mary bears strong resentment towards William regarding their relationship, but she continues to care for him although she sees him very much as the 'dependent child'. Mary will often resort to treating William as 'the naughty child' (for example, if he refuses his food or medication), whereupon William will punch her in the chest. Mary then backs off, but feels both guilty and angry with William that he has not complied with her demands.

The use of abuse as a means of establishing social control is often a way of operating that may be passed down from one generation to the other within a family system and where the gain resulting from a particular situation has secondary implications beyond simply reflecting the situation itself. The above example highlights the gain achieved by William in reinforcing his status within the relationship.

Abuse as a Form of Communication

In the previous section, the use of an abusive act as a means of exerting social control is highlighted as the main reason for perpetrating the act. However, there are circumstances where the intention to control another person's behaviour is secondary to that of communicating their feelings or unmet needs. This is often a function of behaviour in circumstances where the normal channels of communication have been lost or are inaccessible as a result, for example, of physical or mental incapacity or a change in social or environmental circumstances.

The term 'acting out' is often used to denote the function the behaviour is serving. Many therapists, particularly those trained in psychodynamic or psychoanalytic methods, believe that individuals do not simply 'dump' within themselves feelings or unmet needs. Rather, feelings and needs are often repressed, perhaps at an unconscious level, and they are communicated or acted out in some form at particular times or in particular situations. The following example illustrates this function.

Peter and Freda have been married for 60 years. In recent years, however, Freda has been experiencing progressive memory loss as a result of a dementing condition. Whilst Peter continues to care for his wife, he has experienced many losses over the period, in particular his wife's comfort and support during times when he has been feeling stressed or concerned about the future. The loss of support has elicited feelings of anger and resentment in Peter. Although he recognises at 'head level' the reasons for this, emotionally he represses his feelings since he is unable to communicate them in any effective way to his wife since she became ill. At times, Freda may behave in a particularly challenging way which may distress Peter and which will often trigger his repressed feelings, which are expressed as acts of verbal abuse as a way of attempting to communicate his feelings to his wife.

Abuse as a Mechanism for Alleviating Stress

Stress is widely recognised as being both a fundamental feature within many caregiving relationships and a major contribution to a caregiver's ill-health (Twigg & Atkin, 1994; Jones & Peters, 1991; Gilhooly, 1984; Nolan *et al*, 1990; Pearlin *et al*, 1990). It has also been shown as a factor which increases the risk of abuse in some cases (Lau & Kosberg, 1979). Yet, while there has been a wealth of research exploring the factors that are associated with stress, the relationship between stress and abuse is not fully understood. For instance, there are many caregivers who are under considerable stress but who do not perpetrate abuse as a mechanism for stress relief, whereas others may abuse for this purpose. Why should this be the case?

First, the term 'stress' in itself requires qualification. Poulshock & Diemling (1984) suggest that stress has two components: that which relates to the objective changes to a person's bodily functions under conditions of high arousal (stress) and that which reflects a person's experience of themselves in such circumstances (strain). Hence, a person may be under considerable stress physically but not perceive themselves to be so, whilst others may report being under considerable strain but evidence little by way of physical symptoms. Overall, the research evidence suggests that the risk of abuse is higher under conditions of perceived strain than under actual stress.

A second factor relates to coping styles. The more proficient one is in using non-abusive strategies for coping with stress, the less is the likelihood of an abusive act occurring. Coping mechanisms are learned throughout our lives. However, the experience encountered by the child in terms of observing their parents dealing with stress and how they themselves were treated as a focus of stress by them is a significant predictor of abuse in the adult caregiver, particularly where the boundaries of self-control have been broken (Sheilds, 1992; Pruchno & Kleban, 1993)

A third issue relates to the much wider concept of 'meaning'. Here 'meaning' refers to the way in which a person understands or sees the relationship and themselves within that relationship. For example, a caregiver may feel that they are duty bound to provide care for their dependants even though they may not feel comfortable in doing so. In such circumstances, the caregiver is likely to experience further stress and strain as a result of their feelings of resentment, in addition to that experienced from undergoing the various caregiving tasks and pressures inherent within the relationship (Albert, 1992).

Finally, it is widely acknowledged that stress has a compounding or additive effect. That is, where stress is produced by a number of sources, the effect is cumulative. The risk of abuse is increased particularly where the caregiver is unable to cope effectively with the more peripheral stressors. In such cases, a single act perpetrated by the dependant within a caregiving situation may precipitate an act of abuse by virtue of it being 'the straw that breaks the camel's back'. While such an act may give rise to feelings of guilt in the caregiver, it may have a significant gain for them in alleviating stress for that particular moment. In this way, acts of abuse as a form of stress relief are not seen as necessarily premeditated. Rather, they may occur spontaneously. However, it must be noted that abuse occurring as a function of stress accounts for a small proportion of abuse within caregiving contexts.

Abuse as a Way of Resolving Inner Conflicts and Unmet Needs
Many individuals are likely to carry with them a variety of personal problems in their lives. Some of these problems exist as a result of early experiences which are triggered within a relationship at a particular point in time, whilst others may exist as a result of the impact that that relationship is having upon them and which may also be associated with other ongoing current life events.

The Effects of Early Experiences

Many authors have cited the effects that early, aversive experiences can have upon people in their adult lives. Of particular significance are experiences related to abuse and trauma, neglect, over-control by parents or guardians or the effects of regular and painful family disputes. The impact of such experiences can lead to depressed feelings, a diminished view of one's self or identity, poor coping style, negativistic views concerning the value of relationships and over dependency upon others or upon external sources of support (drugs, alcohol and so on). All these factors are likely to play a significant role in the way in which people relate to each other within the caregiving context.

Repressed feelings and needs can be expressed as abusive acts particularly where there is a change in the power position of people within that relationship. The following example illustrates this.

Margaret is a 75-year-old who has experienced several strokes over the past two years. She is being cared for at home by her son John, who has committed a number of acts of sexual abuse upon her throughout this time. John's father died in a road traffic accident when John was about 14 years of age and he has been living with his mother since that time.

In this example, the act of sexual abuse can be seen as serving two main functions for John. First, it served as a way of regaining lost intimacy. In his early years, John neither experienced direct affection from either of his parents nor observed any affection between the two of them. What affection he did experience was via the times when he heard the couple having sex in their bedroom. Secondly, it served as a means of gaining what some therapists describe as 'ego-integrity', that is as a way of enhancing his sexual identity. As a result of never having had close relationships with others, John has had little opportunity to dissociate himself from his mother and thus form an appropriate relationship with her. While there are likely to be many other factors associated with this case, the function the behaviour serves for John is inherent to our understanding why abuse occurs within this context.

A second example reflects the function an abusive act can have as a way of relieving repressed emotions accumulated over many years. Acts of abuse perpetrated for this purpose are termed 'projection' by therapists. The following example illustrates this issue.

Dorothy and Patrick are both in their late seventies and have been married for about 40 years. As a result of a back injury sustained at work, Patrick has been dependent upon Dorothy for many years. This not only resulted in him being unable to gain employment but also affected their social and family lives together. Dorothy's resentment of the circumstances has been building up for many years although she has many positive feelings for Patrick and continues to care for him. She is able to meet many challenges of caregiving, but there are times when she will neglect Patrick's needs for several hours.

In some circumstances, the person to whom the abuse is directed may not have been the original instrument for the perpetrator's difficulties. Rather, they have become what therapists might call an 'object of transference'; that is, the perpetrator's feelings concerning, for example, the parents or the former spouse are being transferred to their dependant, who may not be occupying a similar relationship in the caregiver's life or have characteristics similar to those of past individuals. The gain function the abuse serves in such contexts is nevertheless the same.

The Effects of a Difficult Relationship

While stress and strain is often a major consequence of most caregiving relationships, a second important influence relevant to this section is that of loss. Whether through acute or chronic illness the relationship has become significantly affected, and all parties within that relationship are likely to experience multiple losses. The effects such losses may have upon the well being of those involved will depend upon the value or meaning to individuals of what has been lost (Berg-Cross, 1997).

Of significance within intimate relationships are those losses reflecting affection and value, the sharing of roles, and access to important life experiences, such as social, recreational and spiritual experiences and time to oneself. Such losses are likely to generate a host of unmet needs and distressing feelings for all concerned. Understandably individuals will seek to defend themselves against such losses by denying what has happened and continuing to relate to their partner in a traditional way; or they may actively meet their needs in other ways. In either case, the mechanism for addressing loss in this way, albeit unintentionally, may be through abusive acts. The following example illustrates this issue.

Mary and Bertram have been together for the past 20 years. The couple have children from previous relationships, but they live in different countries and Mary and Bertram see them infrequently. The single most important aspect to the couple's relationship is the value and esteem in which they are held in the local community. In particular, Bertram has been chairman of the local social club and has been influential in funding local community projects.

Unfortunately, Mary was diagnosed as having motor neurone disease some years ago and she is now significantly disabled and relies totally upon Bertram for her care. Although Mary finds going to the social club extremely difficult and undignified, Bertram continues to force her to attend the monthly meetings.

In this example, Bertram has clearly been over-coercive in making Mary attend a social club. His inability to adjust his life around Mary's difficulties can be interpreted as a form of denial or of hanging on to a much-valued past. Bertram is losing not only the Mary he knew and loved but also the wider benefits his partnership held in giving him a sense of meaning and belonging.

Abuse as a Form of Exploitation for Material/Personal Gain
Undoubtedly, there are circumstances within the family or social context where the function of abuse is simply related to a person's desire for material or personal gain. The most salient form of abuse in such circumstances is financial abuse.

Where the gain is considered to be primary, that is, the acquisition of money and property for its own sake, this may be suggestive of several factors. For example, there may be a belief in the perpetrator's mind that their own needs exceed those of the elderly person, or that they somehow have the right to a person's property by virtue of their relationship to that person or of having made personal investment in their care over many years.

However, where the gain is secondary, in that money or property may have a symbolic meaning for the perpetrator rather than purely the value of the property itself, this may be indicative of more long-standing relational difficulties. This is most notable where money and property have been associated with affectional bonding, either in terms of giving money to a relative as a substitute for affection or where aspiring to material gain has been a primary basis for one person valuing another. In the former case, obtaining money or property may be a symbolic way of gaining affection, whereas the latter serves the purpose of affording the perpetrator a sense of self worth.

Finally, there are those who take possession of money or property simply because they see the older person solely as a vessel for personal gain. The need for personal vindication may be irrelevant to the perpetrator.

Unfortunately, illegal access to an older person's finances and property, particularly in the most vulnerable, continues to be an easy option for many people. In part this is due to a lack of adherence to required policies and procedures laid down by financial institutions (Rowe *et al*, 1993) while in other circumstances it may reflect coercing or misleading the older person.

Exercise 6.2
Aim: To enable the reader to consider the concepts outlined in relation to their own practice and clients they have worked with.

Attempt to recount a recent case of abuse that you have been involved in or know about.

1   Try and identify the various gains involved for all parties concerned.
2   What functions did the abuse serve?
3   Would you predict that abuse is likely to continue if nothing changes?

Key Points

1   While social, political, economic, biological or moral issues are important in helping us to understand the basis of abusive behaviour, psychological formulations enable us to develop a model of abusive behaviour upon which therapeutic interventions can be planned.

2   The basic principles of behaviour suggest that:
- behaviour serves a function and is influenced by the gains to the individual which accrue as a consequence of that behaviour;
- behaviour is motivationally driven and is influenced by our needs at the time.

3   Applying the principles of gain with the motivation to abuse, abuse can be seen to serve a number of functions including the following:
- as a way of establishing social control,
- as a form of communication,
- as a mechanism for alleviating stress,
- as a way of resolving inner conflicts and unmet needs,
- as a form of exploitation for material or personal gain,

Suggested Further Reading

Banyard P & Hayes N, 1994, *Psychology! Theory and Application,* Chapman & Hall, London.

Bennett G & Kingston P, 1993, *Elder Abuse, Concepts, Theories and Interventions,* Chapman & Hall, London.

Decalmer P & Glendenning F, 1993, *The Mistreatment of Elderly People,* Sage, London.

Duck S, 1992, *Human Relationships,* 2nd edn, Sage, London.

Fawcett B, Featherstone B, Hearn J & Toft C, 1995, *Violence and Gender Relations, Theories and Interventions,* Sage, London.

Holmes ER & Holmes LD, 1995, *Other Cultures, Elder Years, an Introduction to Cultural Gerontology,* 2nd edn, Sage, London.

Kosberg J, 1983, *Abuse and Maltreatment of The Elderly – Causes and Interventions,* Littleton Wright, Boston.

Lyons RF, Sullivan MJL & Ritvo PG, 1991, *Relationships In Chronic Illness And Disability,* Sage, London.

CHAPTER 7

The Nature of Therapeutic Interventions

Introduction

The term 'therapy' is often likened to the term 'treatment' in the medical sense where an individual has an underlying disease or pathology which requires some form of intervention in order to restore that individual to a state of better health. The term 'cure' is used to denote a positive outcome from that intervention. However, in a psychological sense, therapy does not necessarily imply the presence of an underlying pathology, nor does it imply that cure is a necessary product of therapy. Rather, therapy is seen as a process one goes through where positive change is the outcome. Therapy involves development, or change from one state of circumstances to another.

In a clinical sense, it is assumed that an individual's circumstances are in some way a problem in that the way in which they think, feel or behave is affecting their well-being or quality of life in a manner that is restrictive, distressing or generally unacceptable. This does not in itself imply that there is anything inherently wrong or pathological within the individual per se, but that factors affecting the way in which that individual functions and experiences life are having an effect on their ability to influence their life in a positive way. Simply stated, therapy is the process of change one undertakes which facilitates a better fit to one's life.

Within the field of abuse work, protection of an individual who experiences abuse is not in itself seen as therapeutic. While it may be necessary, in terms both of restricting the opportunity for further physical and psychological deterioration and of enabling time out for change within a client's circumstances to take place, it is the process of change that is considered as the therapeutic agent. Hence, while adult protection procedures may be seen as a necessary element in dealing with abuse, therapeutic intervention is an important component of such a procedure if long-term change is to become an inherent and positive realisation in the life of the client and their family or social network.

A second major issue in understanding therapy within a psychological framework is that it is essentially developed and driven from within the clients themselves. Whereas medical treatments are often applied to individuals who are themselves often passive in their receipt of such treatment, psychological therapies are essentially facilitative, with the client taking a more active role in the change process.

Finally, most medical treatments are specific to the illness they are designed to alleviate. Psychological therapies, however, tend in the main to be specific to the factors which maintain the person's difficulties rather than to the difficulty itself. Hence there is no specific therapeutic intervention for abuse. The type of intervention used depends upon the demonstrated effectiveness of that intervention in dealing with the factors that give rise to abuse, which are likely to be different for each client or case (see previous chapter). Consequently, therapeutic intervention should be based upon a thorough understanding of the abusive context.

In some circumstances, therefore, addressing abuse may involve a discreet intervention, while in others it may necessitate using a range of therapeutic perspectives and procedures possibly incorporating external practical, social and financial support mechanisms if positive change is to take place and be maintained over the long term.

The following section summarises the main types of therapeutic interventions often deployed within abusive contexts either independently or in association with each other. In order to illustrate how much methods may be developed, the following example is cited as a basis for reference.

Joan is 82 years old and has been suffering from a dementing illness for approximately five years. She was widowed ten years ago and until recently had been managing at home with community support. Six months ago, Joan started to wander at night and was found on several occasions walking along her High Street in the early hours of the morning. As a result, Joan's family decided to have Joan stay with them. Joan's family consisted of her daughter Mary, her son-in-law Jack and her grandchildren Simon and Patricia both of whom were in their early twenties. The financial circumstances of the family were rather tight although they were all engaged in either full-time or part time employment.

The nature of Joan's illness made self-care rather difficult for her and she therefore relied exclusively on the support of her family in being able to address issues of personal hygiene, dressing and feeding. While such activities were normally undertaken reasonably well by the family, and without due distress to Joan, the morning routine started to become particularly difficult over a period of several weeks. Specifically, at breakfast time, the family would all sit together, and Mary undertook to feed Joan. However, on various occasions, Joan would refuse to be fed by Mary, which resulted in a build-up of tension and anxiety for Mary and the rest of the family. The pressure on the family needing to leave the house at a particular time and to have Joan ready for her transport which would take her to her day centre often spilled over, whereupon Mary would either over-coerce or, occasionally, physically hit her mother in order to make her accept the food. Although Mary was unhappy at having to use such methods to feed her mother, she nevertheless continued to do so since they resulted in Joan eating her food and the family were therefore able to meet their respective commitments.

Skill Acquisition

Skill acquisition is the process by which an individual is able to learn different or non-abusive ways of achieving a particular task. Used in isolation from other methods, it assumes that the primary factor influencing abusive acts is that the individual has simply not learnt to cope with a particular situation or task without recourse to punitive methods.

The way in which we learn to apply behaviour to a specific situation involves three primary processes: firstly, a behaviour formed effectively in the past is used in the current circumstance to similar effect, and is thereby reinforced; secondly, an individual, having observed someone else behaving in a particular way towards others or indeed towards themselves, performs a similar act within their own set of circumstances; thirdly, insight learning, which focuses upon an individual's ability to solve problems: that is, the ability to abstract from a range of possible approaches or alternatives the one which is likely to have the most beneficial effect in meeting their objective.

These procedures are not mutually exclusive but tend to complement each other in the way in which skills are developed over time. Equally, within the formal process of skills training or skill acquisition all three methods are considered. Skill acquisition involves five primary phases or sessions: orientation, assessment, brainstorming, rehearsal and operation.

Orientation Phase

This phase is intended to help the client focus upon the task in hand and to facilitate a sense of positive action towards accomplishment. It involves (a) establishing rapport with the client and helping them to identify the specific issue or task they wish to accomplish in an environment affording empathy and a non-judgemental approach, (b) providing a full description regarding the following phases, verifying any issues or uncertainties the client may have, and (c) obtaining the client's agreement to commence treatment.

Assessment Phase

The assessment phase, while allowing for wider factors concerning feelings, family relationships and so on to be acknowledged, focuses primarily upon the relationship between the behaviour the client wishes to change, the immediate circumstances or antecedent factors which trigger the behaviour and the consequences that follow the behaviour and which, by definition, have reinforced its continuation throughout. This form of assessment is termed the ABC of behaviour: A = antecedents, B = behaviour and C = consequences.

The most usual approach to gaining this information is by way of an ABC diary which the client is encouraged to complete on a

Table 7.1 *ABC DIARY*
Times when I became pushy with Mum

Date and Time	Description of the circumstances and how I was feeling	What happened?	What were the consequences?
Monday 5 08.30	Breakfast time. I was feeling pressurised and apprehensive.	Mum kept shouting, 'Leave me alone, go away.' She refused her breakfast, so I shouted back and shook her by the shoulders.	Mum was scared, but she eventually let me feed her. I felt guilty but we all managed to leave the house on time.
Tuesday, 6 08.00	Breakfast time. The ambulance had arrived early and Mum wasn't fully dressed. I felt pressure again.	Mum was struggling to put on her clothes. I tried to give her some toast at the same time. It wasn't working. I ended up shouting shouting at her again.	Luckily, the ambulance driver stayed a little longer and I was able to get Mum out. I was late to work and felt angry.
Wednesday, 7 08.30	Breakfast time. I was feeling tired and ill. Mum refused her food again.	I couldn't deal with the situation, so I had my breakfast later and let Mum stay at home. I didn't go to work.	I phoned in sick, again! I felt really guilty that I had let my boss down.
Thursday, 8 08.15	Breakfast time. I was determined that I wasn't going to let my boss down.	Mum was very resistant this morning. I told her to stop behaving like a child and forced her cereal into her mouth. She cried, but took it down.	I felt guilty, but glad that Mum had her breakfast and that we all left on time.

retrospective basis covering the previous two-week period. An example of such a diary is shown in Table 7.1. The information obtained shows us that the trigger factors associated with Mary's over-coercive behaviour in feeding Joan reflects a combination of frustration on Mary's behalf and Joan's reluctance to be fed. The consequences of the behaviour are more often that Joan will then consume her food, which acts as a reinforcer or gain to Mary in that the morning routine is established and her anxieties are reduced. The ABC form could be completed on a prospective basis, but there are ethical implications in doing this in circumstances where the older adult may be exposed to further abuse.

Brainstorming Phase
This phase is designed to help the client come up with a range of alternative coping strategies based upon the information and interpretation drawn from the ABC form. Such strategies may involve those deployed by Mary herself (for example, removing herself from the situation when she feels her anxiety levels are building up and using the period to help herself relax), asking for the assistance of other family members (such as delegating breakfast tasks to other members of the family, thus affording Mary time to be spent exclusively with her mother), or using the support and assistance of outside agencies (such as home care to assist in the morning routine).

The aim of this phase is to brainstorm a range of possible alternatives and to decide which ones are likely to meet the desired outcome in terms of being achievable, realistic and ethical. Once chosen, the desired course of action may necessitate a degree of training or help in its accomplishment. It is important therefore to identify and address the client's needs with a view to successful achievement.

Rehearsal Phase
This phase involves rehearsing the desired course of action as a role-play exercise. Any necessary changes or contingencies are then applied and a plan of action is developed towards implementing the behaviour in the client's natural environment.

Operation Phase

This phase involves implementing the desired course of action and evaluating the need for further changes. It is important to encourage successes and to re-evaluate failures. Where failures have occurred, it may be useful to re-engage the brainstorming phase and follow it through with successive phases of rehearsal and operation (see Table 7.2).

Table 7.2 *Skills Training Procedure*

Phase	Tasks
Orientation	1 Identify target problems 2 Identify desired outcome 3 Support client's motivation towards problem resolution/expectations 4 Describe procedure
Assessment	1 Ascertain functional nature of target problem in terms of: • antecedent conditions/triggers • specific nature/description of problem behaviour • consequences of problem
Brainstorming	1 Ascertain range of possible alternative coping mechanisms (behavioural, cognitive etc) 2 Identify one which is most likely to be beneficial in meeting desired outcome (realistic, achievable, appropriate) 3 Identify and address skills/other needs the client may have in order to accomplish the chosen course of action
Rehearsal	1 Rehearse desired action in a therapeutic context with client (role-play) 2 Make any necessary adjustments
Operation	1 Client to test out designated action in real-life setting 2 Evaluate and support successes, re-evaluate failures (reassess or engage brainstorming phase again) 3 Rehearse changes 4 Implement course of action

Cognitive Therapy

In the previous section, it was shown how various antecedent events can trigger a behaviour. In many cases, the triggering event can reflect a build-up of thoughts the client may have about a situation or individual with whom they are interacting. Such thoughts or 'self-talk' are actually an important component in the process by which we select and control our behaviour. Where self-talk triggers over-controlling or punitive behaviour it is seen as negative, in that it may foster destructive emotions in the individual and have an undesired or destructive effect upon others.

The basis of self-talk is founded upon the attitudes, values and beliefs we may hold towards ourselves and others. These factors are themselves developed throughout our lives, partly in response to those held by our parents or significant others and partly as a direct result of our individual experiences. Cognitive therapy seeks to facilitate positive changes in behaviour by influencing our beliefs and corresponding self talk. There has been a wealth of research into the effectiveness of cognitive therapy, particularly in the field of mental health. There are various methods used in cognitive therapy, most notably reality testing, challenging the rationale of belief systems, refocusing and changing automatic thoughts or 'self-talk' directly (Dryden & Rentoul, 1991).

Reality Testing

This involves comparing the belief concerning a given outcome with the outcome itself and may necessitate the setting up of specific situations and directly exposing the client to those situations. For example, Mary may believe that, if she is unable to feed her mother at the appropriate time, the family will inevitably be late for work, and Joan will also suffer as a result. Fearing both these outcomes and, in addition, that she may experience considerable guilt as a result, Mary's priority is to ensure that Joan eats the breakfast as quickly as possible.

To challenge this belief, the client might be encouraged to explore the validity of her assumptions by working through systematically the various scenarios that might occur were she not to feed her mother and, in addition, to explore the range of alternative outcomes that may be equally apparent. For example, if she is unable to feed her mother,

Joan could be fed by staff at the day centre. Alternatively, should Mary be late for work, her boss might be sympathetic if she were to explain her situation.

Alternatively, Mary could be encouraged to test her predictions directly, for example by being late for work on one occasion. Obviously, discussion would need to take place with the client prior to the experiment being undertaken regarding any contingencies which could be applied in the event that difficulties were incurred.

Challenging the Rationale of the Belief System

Here the therapist may challenge directly the evidence on which the belief has been founded. For example, Mary may believe that her mother whom she is now caring for has begun to resent her efforts. She believes this to be the case as relations between mother and daughter have been difficult for many years. The therapist may wish to offer an alternative explanation for the mother's behaviour in a context of her dementia and thereby to help the client to reframe her interpretation of her mother's resistance: for example, Joan may not recognise her daughter and may therefore interpret her daughter's attempts at feeding her as being threatening. Such a reinterpretation may allow Mary the opportunity to rethink or to establish a different way of operating.

Refocusing

Refocusing involves the direct comparison between one scenario, on which the belief is focused, and another, which holds more positive features. For example, Mary may believe she is totally incompetent at dealing effectively with her pent-up feelings of anger and frustration at times when her mother becomes particularly resistive, in which case recourse to punitive measures may be the only solution. In this example, the therapist would help the client to refocus upon similar situations in the past, for example where their partner or work colleague may have become demanding and ascertain what strategies were used in those contexts, which she may be able to use in the current circumstances.

Changing Automatic Thoughts or 'Self-Talk' Directly
There are various forms of automatic thoughts which can be identified, including the following:

- arbitrary inference, for example, 'She didn't say thank you, therefore she doesn't love me';
- selective abstraction, for example, 'He takes me for granted because he is always watching the television';
- over-generalisation, for example, 'he can't understand what I am trying to do, he never will';
- magnification, for example, 'I just can't get her to dress herself, maybe I should give up completely';
- minimisation, for example, 'I managed to dress her, but then anyone could if they worked at it';
- personalisation, for example, 'He won't eat his dinner because he hates me';
- dichotomous reasoning, for example, 'I keep making mistakes, therefore I should not be doing this any more'.

The process for addressing automatic thoughts involves assisting the client in identifying thoughts that arise in specific situations, challenging the thoughts directly or via the belief systems on which they are founded, and encouraging the client to practise alternative thoughts. For example, Mary would be asked to record the thoughts that come into her mind at times when she is feeding her mother and in particular when her mother becomes resistive to feeding.

The client is assisted to develop their own process for undertaking this procedure, usually by keeping a diary where, following a series of similar situations, they would write down what automatic thoughts came into their mind. Then, they are encouraged to challenge the basis of these thoughts and identify what alternative thoughts they could generate which would be more appropriate in eliciting positive coping strategies. Where alternative thoughts precipitate adaptive behaviour, that is successful outcomes, then this is likely to affect the client's underlying belief systems in a positive way.

Below, we consider a different example:

Dermott is the primary caregiver of his father, Mr O'Connor. Father and son live together in the family home. Mr O'Connor has recently suffered a stroke which has limited his mobility and ability to care for himself. Emotionally, Mr O'Connor is very angry and frustrated at his loss of independence and does not take too kindly to having others assist him in his personal care. Dermott has always considered his father a stubborn and obstinate man, who has become exceedingly more so since his stroke. When Dermott attempts to help his father dress, the following automatic thoughts are elicited: 'I hate having to do this, I know that he is going to be a bloody pain. I am not going to be able to cope with him, especially this morning. If he causes me hassle, I'm going to throttle him'.

In the therapeutic session, the therapist would ask the client to generate those thoughts as if he was back in the situation. The client would then be encouraged to generate a range of alternative thoughts which would be more productive, aimed at re-addressing his feelings, reframing his father's behaviour and developing alternative coping strategies in the event of Mr O'Connor becoming difficult: for example, 'I'm not going to get pent up'; 'Maybe today he will not become such a pain'; 'I will take one step at a time'; 'If he does become threatening, I'll just say "Okay" and walk away'.

The automatic thoughts may then be practised within the session and evaluated as to suitability and acceptability for the client. Once this strategy has been mastered, the client will try it out several times in the real-life situation, using a diary format. Obviously, one would expect failures during the initial phase, so the client may require significant levels of support and encouragement during this period.

Individual Psychotherapy

Simply stated, the term 'psychotherapy' can be defined as the treatment of psychological disorders by psychological methods. The term could be applied to the methods of therapists skilled in any single or multiple approaches in psychological treatments, but, in practice, psychotherapy tends to be used in those situations requiring more dynamic work and should therefore only be undertaken by those with accredited training and qualifications.

Psychotherapy is primarily aimed at those individuals whose capacity to lead independent and fulfilling lives is restricted by internal emotional conflicts and whose view of themselves is likely to be diminished. In such cases, individuals are likely to experience severe emotional stress across a range of circumstances (usually in intimate relationships) and may resort to using self-harm, neglect or self-punishment, or abuse projected upon others as a means of coping or responding to personal experiences.

The causes or influences which give rise to such circumstances are often rooted in an individual's early experiences where, through trauma, prolonged emotional deprivation or repeated failure, the personal foundations for growth and well-being in adulthood have not been developed. Through the process of conflict resolution, mediated by specific aspects inherent in the therapeutic relationship, the client is encouraged to take personal responsibility for themselves and their actions, to take appropriate risks in facing life's challenges and to develop a sense of unconditional self-worth.

The processes often used in psychotherapy depend upon the theoretical orientation of the therapist (Rogerian, Gestalt, Psychoanalytic and so on) and may include facilitating emotional expression, redirecting feelings of anger, bereavement counselling, self-nurturing activities, confidence building, problem solving and self-awareness. Inherent within the psychotherapeutic process is the importance given to the so called 'non specific' aspects of therapy: that is, the provision of warmth, empathy, acknowledgement and unconditional positive regard.

Couple Counselling

Couple counselling involves the application of psychological theories and procedures aimed at assisting couples to develop their relationship in a productive way. While counselling draws upon theories and methods used in psychotherapy, its remit is primarily developmental rather than purely therapeutic. That is, whereas psychotherapeutic and related procedures may be applied to the more severe range of human difficulties (depression, long-standing personality disorders and so on) necessitating a treatment-oriented approach, counselling approaches are more specifically applied to ordinary problems of daily living where individuals are seen as having the potential within themselves to alleviate their difficulties without recourse to more intensive treatment.

The approach is essentially facilitative, deploying a variety of methods and theoretical frameworks to assist couples in open communication and expression of feelings, and helping them to identify and challenge defences, assert themselves within the relational context, explore their needs and motivations, and to acknowledge each other's feelings. Finally this approach helps to develop opportunities for problem solving and risk taking and for activities which enhance the well-being of the couple.

Whereas many treatment-oriented methods tend to identify their outcomes from the start, counselling approaches seek to encourage the client to develop and work towards their own agenda. Consequently, outcomes following counselling are likely to be varied. In some cases, termination of the relationship rather than its continuation, may be an appropriate course of action for the couple to have taken. What is important is that the decision to terminate or continue has been developed, accepted and chosen by the couple themselves.

A major consideration in receiving clients for counselling is the extent to which both parties are willing and able to contribute to the therapeutic process. Both the onus and accountability for change lie primarily with the couple, rather than with the counsellor or the wider therapeutic system. In circumstances where the 'power position' to influence the relationship is biased in favour of one party (for example, in cases of dementia where the caregiver holds the balance of power), careful consideration would need to be given before deciding that this counselling approach is the most appropriate course of action.

Family Therapy

Family therapy is not in itself a distinctive therapeutic method. Rather, it is a term which is used to denote several therapeutic orientations that seek to understand human functioning in systemic rather than purely individual terms. That is, it views the family not as a collection of individuals but as a system whose way of operating is a product of the interrelationship between family members, their wider social, cultural and environmental attachment and the influence family generations have upon each other.

Furthermore, family therapy would consider individual problems as reflecting either 'symptoms' of that family's underlying difficulties (such as problems of communication) or as their 'solutions' in dealing with those difficulties. For example, an individually oriented therapist might view Mary's difficulties in assisting her dependent mother with feeding as related to poor coping style or as a function of chronic stress, while the family therapist might view the situation as either symptomatic of the wider family's attempt to deal with the difficulties brought about as a result of Joan entering the family system, or as their solution in dealing with difficulties they may have had prior to Joan entering the system.

Consequently, intervention is unlikely to highlight any single individual. Rather, it will be focused upon assisting the whole family in re-establishing a way of operating which considers much wider aspects of the family's structure, dynamics and interrelationships. In attempting to understand the family in systemic terms, family therapists deploy the terms 'hierarchy and boundaries', 'role flexibility', 'congruent communication', 'goodness of fit', and 'differentiation'.

Hierarchy and Boundaries
This refers to the various status positions each member of the family might hold and what are deemed permissible or non-permissible courses of action in the way in which individuals relate to one another. While boundaries are important in both protecting and delineating family relationships, boundaries need to change as the family undergoes various changes throughout the course of its development. However, there are circumstances in which boundaries are inappropriately broken (for example, in cases of sexual abuse between adult child and parent) or where boundaries do not exist at all (for example, where parent–child relationships become enmeshed). Such circumstances can often be a major cause of conflict and dysfunction within family systems.

Role Flexibility
This refers to the extent to which individuals within the family system are able to undertake specific roles. Many individuals, especially

caregivers themselves, may be required to undertake roles and responsibilities which they are not used to or which may compromise their status and identity within the relationship, as when, for example, a spouse has to learn to cook for their dependant. Problems in role flexibility can often give rise to severe stress.

Congruent Communication

Congruent communication refers to the nature and extent to which family members are able to communicate with each other in a meaningful and compatible way. Poor communication can often lead to misinterpretation of people's actions, desires or expectations and limit the extent to which effective interaction can take place.

Goodness of Fit

The term 'fit' reflects the extent to which a family is compatible, in terms of life styles, attitudes, social behaviour and so on, with the social environment in which it functions. Goodness of fit enables a family's need for self-identity and meaningful existence to be met. In cases where a family may be functioning within a context that is incompatible with goodness of fit, this can prove a particular obstacle to adaptive functioning, as where, for example, a family has to relocate to a community operating different social, cultural and political standards. In such cases, conflicts can arise between family members where abusive acts can be seen as symptomatic of the stresses and strains the family is encountering in attempting to adjust to new circumstances.

Differentiation

The term 'differentiation' is used to denote the degree of growth and maturity of family systems. A differentiated system is one which is open to its social and material environment and will use its resources, information and opportunities to resolve problems and maintain a sense of harmony or 'homeostasis'. An undifferentiated system holds to rigid boundaries and practices, which often gives rise to abusive behaviour as a means of maintaining social control.

According to Giordano & Giordano (1984), there are a number of salient features evident in undifferentiated systems where abuse is most likely to occur:

- where violence is a normative pattern of behaviour across generations;
- where there exists a high level of demand stress;
- where there are defined personality problems inherent in the perpetrator;
- where there may exist unresolved relational conflicts, for example between parent and child;
- where there exist further external stresses imposed, for example, by the environment, wider family networks, work or illness of the caregiver;
- where negative attitudes towards a dependant proliferate to such an extent as to suppress guilt where abusive situations arise;

The procedure for intervention depends upon the outcome of assessment (which is itself considered to be a part of the therapeutic process) and calls upon a range of methods, some of which are exclusive to family therapy while others are similar to individual-based approaches. Broadly speaking, intervention helps the family to reframe or restate the 'problem' in terms that make it solvable and which enable the family to move towards a more differentiated way of operating through developments in boundary setting, problem solving, congruent communication and resource generation. The following example illustrates this approach.

Mrs Thomas was admitted to hospital for rehabilitation following a succession of falls. Clinical investigation diagnosed vascular dementia but, while the falls might have reasonably been attributed to the effects of the illness, the nature of her bruises was considered inconsistent with falling.

Regarding the family circumstances, Mrs Thomas lived at home, being cared for primarily by her youngest child, Kate (unmarried, late fifties) but is also supported by two other children (themselves married and living some distance away). During several interviews with the family, they disclosed the difficulties they were experiencing in caring for their mother: in particular, Kate was considered to be under enormous stress.

While actual abuse was never disclosed either by the patient or by the family, it was the team's opinion that there were sufficient grounds to infer abuse. An initial review meeting was held by the immediate members of the team, the outcome of which was to commence adult protection procedures. The senior social worker undertook to hold a case conference, which was attended by all members of the family and included relevant team members from the hospital and those providing community support. As a result of the case conference, the issue regarding the patient's immediate need for protection and care was covered, as the medical officer was prepared to keep Mrs Thomas in hospital until suitable discharge arrangements were made. In addition, the issue of family therapy was discussed with the family in order to help them explore further issues in the care of their mother. The family agreed to this approach and a series of sessions were devoted to this purpose.

View of the family system

Essentially, the dynamics appeared to suggest a rather 'closed' family, but one which evidenced a degree of differentiation in terms of status, roles and geographical boundaries. The primary responsibility for caregiving was held by Kate, with some practical and emotional support offered by her older siblings.

The relationship between Kate and her mother was considered a primary source of conflict in that Kate had not undergone a successful transition. That is, while she was able to intellectualise the changes in her mother's personality, she was still emotionally dependent upon her mother for both support and attention. As this was no longer available to Kate in her interactions with her mother, her intense feelings of hurt or anger were probably acted out in the form of spontaneous physical aggression. Nevertheless, Kate's decision to continue in her role was acknowledged.

Progress of intervention
The first session allowed for a free expression of feelings between all members of the family which itself displayed close emotional bonds between individuals. Kate disclosed her own feelings towards her mother and her siblings and became aware of the enormous difficulties she was experiencing in coming to terms with the changes that had taken place in her mother's personality. In addition, the adult children, including Kate, were encouraged to declare openly their own strengths and limitations in supporting their mother, and to disclose what they were prepared to offer.

At the second session family members disclosed that they had continued their discussions with each other and that they were happy to explore a number of possible solutions. As a result, the following courses of actions were proposed:

- provision of day care for Mrs Thomas which would assist in both supporting her social, psychological and physical well being and offering valuable respite for Kate;
- Kate was to receive individual therapy in order to address the issues of transition in the relationship between herself and her mother;
- home care was to be provided to assist in both the practical and management of Mrs Thomas and in offering continuous support to Kate;
- access to a carer support group, including direct access to the case worker if required, was to be available for any member of the family;
- the provision of a respite bed was also included to act both as a contingency in the event of a crisis and as a planned respite (two-week block) for the purpose of extended breaks or holidays for Kate.

Outcome
A further five sessions were carried out over a period of approximately 12 months. At the end of this period, Mrs Thomas was eventually admitted to full-time residential care, as the family members felt it was a more appropriate basis for continuing their relationship without having to become enmeshed with the role of caregiving. Kate herself undertook individual treatment throughout this period, during which

the issues of loss, unmet expectations and unresolved conflicts were addressed; but the treatment also offered her the ability to engage in new and successful relationships with others. There was no evidence of any further abuse throughout this period.

Exercise 7.1

Mr and Mrs Fitzpatrick are a couple both in their late seventies. Mrs Fitzpatrick has been suffering from a dementing condition for about two years. Some three months ago, the couple moved in with their son and daughter-in-law, who live in a three-bedroomed semi-detached house together with their son, Phillip. Phillip is 20 years old and has a learning disability. Mr and Mrs Fitzpatrick have had a rather stormy relationship for many years.

During the first month following Mr and Mrs Fitzpatrick's moving in with their son and daughter-in-law, the whole family seemed to operate very well together, sharing in instrumental and affectional exchanges with each other. However, about two months ago, Phillip developed a close relationship with a female whom he invited for Sunday lunch at the family home. During lunch, Mrs Fitzpatrick accused Phillip's friend of being a prostitute and a thief. The family were shaken and embarrassed at Mrs Fitzpatrick's sudden outburst and, in an attempt to silence his wife, Mr Fitzpatrick struck her across the face. As a consequence, Phillip started to shout and threw his cutlery at the couple, eventually leaving the room. This lead Phillip's mother to break down in tears and her son began to have angry exchanges with both his parents.

The following weeks were fraught with tension and Phillip retired to his bedroom. In addition, Mr and Mrs Fitzpatrick had frequent arguments, and on occasion Mr Fitzpatrick physically assaulted his wife. As a result, the son and daughter-in-law eventually sought advice from their general practitioner.

Scenario 1

The general practitioner refers the daughter-in-law to you for help in overcoming her stress-related difficulties. Adopting a purely skilled training-based approach, how would you set about helping her?

Scenario 2

The general practitioner refers Mr Fitzpatrick for assistance in dealing with his anger towards his wife. Adopting a cognitive behavioural approach, how would you set about helping him?

Scenario 3

Phillip is referred to you for assistance in coping with his emotional lability. Reflecting upon methods of emotional control, how would you set about helping him?

Scenario 4

The whole family is referred to you for assistance in achieving a more harmonious way of operating together. With the information given above, answer the following:

- What assumptions do you think are being made in the referral request?
- What are the main themes or system constructs you would wish to explore in developing a formulation of the family's functioning?
- How would you assist the family in reframing their problems in a manner which lends itself to intervention?
- What issues would you predict the family are likely to raise as priorities for help?

Finally, it may be helpful to explore your own thoughts and feelings concerning the family:

- Does the above example trigger any thoughts or feelings relating to your own family or experiences?
- Are you aware of any stereotypes or prejudices you may have which come through in your understanding of the family or the difficulties they have?

- What would you consider to be your strengths and weaknesses in addressing each scenario?

Key points

1 Intervention strategies vary in accordance with client definition (the individual, the subsystem or couple, or the wider family system) and the theoretical orientation of the therapist.
2 Methods include those which are specifically focused upon one area of functioning or those which involve multiple levels of functioning.
3 Discrete methods include:

- behavioural skills training, aimed at the development of alternative coping strategies intended to replace abusive behaviour;
- cognitive restructuring, aimed at changing maladaptive thinking styles affecting the selection and control of behaviour through challenging the rationale of belief systems, refocusing, re-attribution and changing automatic thoughts;
- developing emotional control aimed at controlling times of heightened emotion which often acts as a trigger for abusive behaviour.

4 Integrated methods include:

- individual psychotherapy, aimed at addressing issues related to unresolved conflicts, depreciated self-image and global personality difficulties;
- couple counselling, aimed at helping couples or subsystems to address relational discord and to develop their relationship in a productive way;
- family therapy, which applies the principles of the systems theory to assisting families in their development without their having recourse to abusive interactions where such interactions may be construed as symptomatic of wider difficulties or as the family's 'solution' in dealing with such difficulties. Central to the framework of family therapy are the constructs of hierarchy and boundaries, role flexibility, congruent communication, differentiation and goodness of fit.

Suggested Further Reading

Berg-Cross L, 1997, *Couples Therapy,* Sage, London.

Browne K & Herbert M, 1992, *Preventing Family Violence,* John Wiley, Chichester.

Burnard P, 1994, *Counselling Skills for Health Professionals*, 2nd edn, Chapman & Hall, London.

Duck S & Wood JT, 1995, *Confronting Relationship Challenges,* Sage, London.

Hansson RO & Carpenter BN, 1994, *Relationships in Old Age: Coping with the Challenge of Transition,* The Guilford Press, New York.

Heron J, 1990, *Helping The Client – A Creative Practical Guide*, Sage, London.

Neidhardt ER & Allen JA, 1992, *Family Therapy with the Elderly,* Sage, Thousand Oaks.

Parker G, 1993, *With this Body: Caring and Disability in Marriage,* Open University Press, Buckingham.

Ponterotto JG, 1995, *Handbook of Multicultural Counselling*, Sage, Thousand Oaks.

Pritchard J, 1999, *Elder Abuse Work, Best Practice in Britain and Canada,* Jessica Kingsley, London

Resick P & Schnicke M, 1993, *Cognitive Processing Therapy for Rape Victims: A Treatment Manual,* Sage, Thousand Oaks.

Part 3

Abuse within Family Settings

CHAPTER 8

Family Relationships

Introduction

In Chapter 4, the importance of the family for the emotional well-being of older people was highlighted. It is recognised that the family fulfils a number of functions in later life, which include the following:

- a sense of relatedness with the world, when other opportunities such as work are reduced;
- maintenance of a sense of self-worth and self-esteem;
- the provision of valued roles;
- the provision of emotional warmth and openness;
- a source of caring in the event of ill-health.

In spite of research in support of the above, the prevailing myth surrounding families is that they no longer care about their elders and that, consequently, older people are abandoned by their families. Research into the numbers of older people who live with family members has shown however, that 64 per cent of older people still live with one family member (Jarvis, 1993) and even for those who live alone it cannot be assumed that the family does not care (Victor, 1991).

Qureshi & Walker (1989) amongst others, highlight the complex nature of older people's living arrangements which, while clearly demonstrating that older people are increasingly living separately from their children and other relatives, dispels the myth mentioned above. The contacts that older people have with family are frequently complex, considerable and involve much potential for reciprocity. With increasing research available, elder abuse as a form of family violence can no longer be denied. As has already been outlined, family violence towards older people takes many forms and can be a cause of considerable distress to the older person. The simplistic view, that abuse arises from circumstances in which an elder is placing increasing demands on a caregiver, which results in increased stress, is not only inappropriate but it denies the complexity of the circumstances in which abuse occurs and tends to blame the victim. This chapter is therefore concerned with informing the reader of the dynamics of family relationships as well as the factors and individuals within families that give rise to abuse. Following a discussion of these factors, the issue of gaining access to and assessing older people in suspected abusive situations is explained.

It is argued by Pillemer (1993) that the view that abuse only arises out of situations in which the older person has a need of care contributes to the maintenance of the stressed caregiver hypothesis. He further suggests that research has demonstrated that only a small percentage of abuse occurs in caregiving situations, and that the abuser is unlikely to be the caregiver. However, the research referred to is primarily American, and this view has not been validated by research in the United Kingdom. While it is important to accept that abuse is more likely to arise as a consequence of the nature of dependence of the person who perpetrates the abuse on the older person (for example, for financial gain), there is a need to acknowledge that the abuse encountered by practitioners is likely to be within the context of interventions as a result of the older person's need for care. This should not be seen as a validation of the stressed caregiver hypothesis, only a recognition of the context within which practitioners are likely to come into contact with an older person.

Many UK authors have argued that focusing on the abuser rather than the dependent is the most appropriate basis for intervention in abusive situations (Homer & Gilleard, 1990; Bennett & Kingston, 1993; Nolan, 1993). The theories outlined in Chapter 2 identify current thinking on why abuse occurs, and reinforce the need for a shift in focus. However, it seems clear from these theories that abuse arises from both interpersonal and intrapersonal issues, which require further exploration.

Exercise 8.1
Aim: to facilitate an increased knowledge of the interpersonal and intrapersonal factors that may create circumstances in which abuse occurs.

Having worked through the book to this point, it is likely that you will have identified families or individuals that you have had involvement with where you suspect abuse or neglect has occurred or is occurring. Identify the factors that raised your suspicions and discuss them with a colleague if possible. Compare them with the following information.

Interpersonal Factors

Abuse within families occurs within the context of the relationship, whether that is a couple, a parent and child or a larger family unit. It is therefore necessary to understand the nature of family relationships and the ways in which families relate as a system. Neidhardt & Allen (1993) amongst others, suggest that 'thinking family' is an important concept for practitioners working with an older person, as it enables us to develop a wider view of the situation, and therefore direct interventions more effectively. These authors go on to suggest that there are significant reasons why a systemic approach should be utilised when working with older people within the context of their families.

---

1. Difficulties in any part of the relationship system may give rise to symptomatic expression in other parts of the system.
2. Symptomatic relief at one part of the system may result in a transfer of symptomatic expression to another site.
3. Significant change ... in any part of the system may result in change in other parts of the system.

(Keeney, 1979 p120; cited in Neidhardt & Allen, 1993).

A systemic perspective allows the practitioner to recognise the behaviour patters within the family that give rise to abusive behaviour. Furthermore, it is recognised that families need to be viewed in the context of the life stage they are at, which also gives rise to various transitions which in themselves may contribute to the risk of abusive behaviour, such as retirement or the need for care (Carter & McGoldrick, 1989).

The ways that families relate can be viewed in the context of a number of concepts which are relevant to family-centred practice (Neidhardt & Allen, 1993). They are discussed here as a basis for understanding the interpersonal factors which contribute to the risk of abuse.

Dependency

In Chapter 2, the theory that dependency is a causative factor in elder abuse was discussed. Because of the persistence of the stressed caregiver hypothesis, it appears that, in an attempt to refute it, the argument over dependency has been polarised, with the focus being switched to the abuser. Research suggests that the abuser is dependent upon the older person, usually for finances and often for housing (Pillemer, 1993), and also that task demands as a factor in their own right associated with caregiving are not a causative factor in elder abuse.

However, the onset of the need for care, or retirement, creates a need to change the way that relationships function. In systemic terms, the boundaries and hierarchies are diffused in dependent relationships, and the roles are likely to be rigidly defined. This leads to circumstances in which the ability to encompass new roles is likely to create conflict and mental ill-health, both of which have been found to increase the risk of elder abuse (Bendick, 1992; Pillemer & Suitor, 1992) (see Chapter 7 for further discussion of systems theory).

Transgenerational Violence

It was highlighted in Chapter 2 that the transgenerational violence theory requires further exploration. MacEwen (1994) has researched this in relation to family violence as a whole. This study has tentatively found that this hypothesis is likely to be true, but MacEwen qualifies this: 'There are features of the original learning situation that contribute to the prediction of current aggression, over and above the mere occurrence of family of origin' (p361).

This study appears to have found that a past history of aggression, in itself, is not a predictor of current family violence unless the following factors are present:

1   Both the experiences of aggression and witnessed aggression in the family of origin exert cumulative effects on current relationship aggression.
2   Past experience of aggression in the family of origin is more likely to be predictive of current relationship aggression when the original experience had a significant negative impact.
3   The extent to which the individual identifies with the original aggressor predicts the extent of the current relationship aggression.

Homer & Gilleard (1990) also found evidence to support this theory. In their study, many of the couples had a long history of an abusive relationship: the abuse was not a recent experience. Both study samples were small and are therefore not generalisable; however, they highlight some interesting results which require further research. The research discussed emphasises the need to explore the family history, and to assess the extent to which aggression was the norm within the families' ways of coping.

Intrapersonal Factors
Many intrapersonal factors have been highlighted as predictors of abuse, which reinforce the appropriateness of focusing on the abuser. Furthermore, these factors validate the use of assessment procedures that utilise psychological frameworks to elucidate the causes of abuse. The following factors have been highlighted in research in both the UK and the United States.

1   History of mental illness, including mood disturbance (Homer & Gilleard, 1990; Bendik, 1992; Wolf 1994; Pillemer & Finkelhor, 1989).
2   External locus of control, believing events are outside of one's control (Bendik, 1992).
3   Lacking problem solving skills (Bendik, 1992; Pillemer & Finkelhor, 1989).
4   Alcohol or substance misuse (Homer & Gilleard, 1990; Wolf, 1994).
5   Life crisis, such as onset of ill-health or bereavement (Pillemer & Finkelhor, 1989; Hamilton, 1989).

6   Inadequate social supports (Bendik, 1992; Pillemer & Finkelhor, 1989).

These factors do not act in isolation; rather, a number of these are present and lead to circumstances in which they act together to create conditions where abuse arises. They are further heightened by such factors as experience of violence from the older person (Pillemer & Suitor, 1992; Paveza *et al*, 1992) and income inadequacy (Bendik, 1992).

It is therefore recognised that the risk factors for abuse within families are multifaceted, and are likely to be a consequence of the past relationships of the family members, their relational competence and intrapersonal factors, which give rise to conflict when circumstances occur which require a change in the ways that the family interact.

Further research has recently begun to explore whether certain risk factors are associated with certain types of abuse and neglect. The following factors seemed to arise.

Physical and Psychological Abuse
Elder: physically well, but has emotional problems, may be violent towards the abuser.
Abuser: history of alcoholism, and/or mental illness; is more likely to live with the victim and is financially dependent upon them. Is the spouse of the victim and has high conflict with the victim. If not a spouse, may be experiencing the above and significant life stressors. There is a history of a previously poor relationship, with evidence of past unresolved conflicts and, possibly, violence (Wolf & Pillemer, 1989; Wolf, 1994; Homer & Gilleard, 1990).

Financial Abuse
Elder: Unmarried, with limited social networks.
Abuser: has financial problems, which may be traceable to a history of substance abuse (Wolf & Pillemer, 1989).

Sexual Abuse
Elder: usually dependent on the abuser for care; more likely to be female and to have a degree of mental impairment.

Abuser: usually male, either a husband or son (Ramsey Klawsnik, 1991).

Neglect
Elder: very old and has both mental and physical impairment.
Abuser: finds the victim a great source of stress, and does not have the coping strategies to respond to the care needs of the elder. Evidence of poor relationship (Wolf & Pillemer, 1989; Homer & Gilleard, 1990).

Much of the research that has been drawn upon is American in origin, and as a consequence further research is required to explore the relevance of these findings to the UK. Homer & Gilleard's work (1990) seems to suggest that the experience of abuse in the UK may have some similarities with that of the United States, and, although it is small-scale, their paper clearly points the way for further research.

Access and Assessment
It is essential for any practitioner who is working with older people to have a sound knowledge of elder abuse. This should include an awareness of the risk factors identified above, so that they may be alert to these when assessing clients and their families. However, it is obviously not as simple as that: gaining access and assessing for abuse and neglect involve considerable skill and sensitivity. The older person rarely alleges elder abuse, so that gaining access to assess for the presence of abuse or neglect requires careful consideration and planning. Some of the barriers to access have already been referred to, it is useful at this point to consider them more fully.

Barriers from the older person
- They may fear further retaliation from the abuser.
- They may believe that any intervention will separate them from their family.
- They may not perceive the situation as abusive.
- They may be unable to give consent to access and assessment because of illness or impairment of physical or cognitive functioning or communication.

- They may perceive professional involvement as interfering and invasive.
- They may feel that they deserve the abuse as a consequence of their dependence.
- They may be ashamed or embarrassed.

Responses to barriers are discussed further in Chapter 10. However, it is clear that, for some of these barriers, empowering the older person, by informing them of their rights to be free from abuse, as described by Breckman & Adelman (1988) in their staircase model of intervention, is an important first step in gaining the confidence of the older person. Where competence to give consent to access and assessment is an issue, the rights of the older person need to be balanced with their right to protection before steps to gain access are taken. In any event, as Breckman & Adelman (1988) state, 'Attempts at access need to be tailored to each individual case and the success will depend on the degree of resistance on the part of the abuser and victim' (p40).

Access arrangements should be planned beforehand, with consideration given not only to the safety of the older person, but also to the safety of the worker. It may well be necessary to go to the house in pairs. This may be useful in that it will provide an opportunity to assess the older person and the person who is alleged to be perpetrating the abuse (if they are present) separately. Breckman & Adelman (1988) further argue that access is often achieved by an 'understanding of the available options, persistency and tenacity'. Assessment should aim to achieve the following:

- Consistent with Johnson's definition, outlined in Chapter 2, assessment should aim to determine the level of risk that the older person is facing, that is, the density (number of types of abuse) and intensity (the frequency of the abuse).
- Assessment which is as comprehensive as possible, but which should also seek to follow the principle of being the least invasive possible.
- Assessment of the ability of the older person to make competent decisions about their situation.
- Understanding of the older person's view of the situation, and the

reasons why the abuse occurs, this would also facilitate an assessment of intent.

• The support networks and resources available to the older person.
• A clear assessment of the person alleged to perpetrate the abuse, and the extent to which they are involved with the older person (Breckman & Adelman, 1988).

In addition to the above, any guidelines produced for either adult protection or elder abuse within the reader's authority may well give details on the information that is required.

The actual process of assessment, in relation to the techniques utilised to gain information, will depend to a certain extent on the professional background of the assessor. Certain skills, such as the use of active listening, probing, open and closed questioning, observation and paraphrasing, will be common to many practitioners. In addition, the practitioner should guard against the use of leading questions, as any information gained could be used in legal proceedings against the abuser. There are certain tools available which can guide the assessor in assessment. The reader is referred to Bennett & Kingston (1993) and Decalmer & Glendenning (1993) for a description of some of these. The tools help provide a useful framework for assessment, and for systematic recording; however, they cannot and should not be relied upon totally. The creativity and flexibility of the assessor are of key importance.

Exercise 8.2
Aim: To facilitate critical thinking around the principles and practice of assessment. Read through the following case examples.

Case Study 1
Mr Parsons is a 79-year-old who lives in a sheltered complex. He has lived there for six months, following a fire at his house caused by faulty wiring. His son persistently complains that he is unsafe, that he has become confused and aggressive towards him and is wandering at night. He has approached his family doctor to ask for his father to be admitted to hospital. Mr Parsons receives care from a local agency three times a week. The warden is concerned about

him, as he has noticed a deterioration in his psychological health: he has become depressed and withdrawn and is very guarded when his son arrives to visit him. The home care agency has noticed that he frequently has no money and has limited food supplies in the house. When asked by the warden if anything is wrong, he denies there are any problems.

Case Study 2
Mrs Ravinder Kaur arrives in your unit for a two-week period of respite. She speaks little English and has significant physical disabilities. She is cared for at home by her son and daughter-in-law, and they have gone on holiday. The unit has a policy that all clients have a medical assessment on their first day. On examination, the doctor finds significant bruising around Mrs Kaur's inner thighs, her upper arms and her back. The staff say that the family made them aware of the bruising, saying that she was persistently falling as a consequence of poor mobility.

Having read through the case studies, and choose one of them to answer the following questions:

1   What factors might lead you to suspect that abuse or neglect is occurring?
2   Which professionals should be involved in the assessment process?
3   What barriers to access might there be?
4   What would be your plan to assess the situation?
5   List the questions you might use to determine whether abuse is occurring or not.

Key Points
1   When there is a suspicion that abuse or neglect is occurring, the circumstances are rarely defined and they require a comprehensive and multidisciplinary assessment.
2   Assessment should be holistic, but should start by obtaining the views of the older person on what they wish to happen.

3   Consistent with the need to focus on interventions which do not contribute to the abuse which the older person has already experienced, the abuser should be interviewed to determine the causative factors and the level of risk of recurrence. Interventions should then be planned accordingly.

4   Assessment should be planned, and assessors need to be creative and patient in their approach, considering how and when an assessment should take place. Due consideration needs to be given to where assessment will take place, to ensure privacy and to offer protection to the older person.

5   All information gained should be systematically recorded, even if the older person refuses intervention. This is for both professional and legal purposes.

6   Assessment should seek to obtain information about the competence of the older person to make decisions about the level of risk they are exposed to.

7   Even if intervention is refused, agreement to some form of regular contact could be reached with the older person.

Suggested Further Reading

Bennett GC & Kingston P, 1993, *Elder Abuse – Concepts Theories and Interventions*, Chapman & Hall, London.

Breckman RS & Adelman RD, 1988, *Strategies for Helping Victims of Elder Mistreatment*, Sage, Thousand Oaks.

Davies M, 1993, 'Recognising Abuse: An Assessment Tool for Nurses' in Decalmer P & Glendenning F (eds) *The Mistreatment of Elderly People,* Sage, London.

Decalmer P *et al,* 1993, 'The Multi-Disciplinary Assessment of Clients and Patients' in Decalmer P & Glendenning F (eds) *The Mistreatment of Elderly People*, Sage, London.

Wolf RS & Pillemer K, 1989, *Helping Elderly Victims, The Reality of Elder Abuse*, Columbia University Press, New York.

CHAPTER 9

Working with Families

Introduction

Unlike abuse perpetrated by outsiders, abuse within the family has its own special considerations. These include understanding the factors which give rise to and maintain abusive behaviour, the impact abuse has for the victim and their wider family members, and the implications these issues have for therapeutic involvement. Thus the family is a distinct and unique context within which to apply therapeutic interventions, for several reasons,

Firstly, the family is not simply a combination of individuals held together by discrete linear relationships. Rather, it is an active and dynamic system characterised by a continuous interactive style involving circular relationships, where changes to one part of the system promote reactions in every other part of that system.

Secondly, the family is not simply influenced by a single life transition as with, for example, an individual who may be experiencing difficulties adjusting from their role as an adult child to that of caregiver. Rather, the family as a whole may be experiencing multiple transitions either exclusively (for example, during periods of relocation) or as a product of multiple transitions experienced by individual family members (for example, in the adoption of new roles and responsibilities). At times, a family's life-cycle stage may blend with those of its individual members; at other times, it may be dissonant.

Thirdly, families do not exist in a vacuum. They are both influenced by and dependent upon the culture in which they operate and survive.

In addressing abuse within the family context, it is therefore important that interventions are applied from the basis of systems theory (Neidhardt & Allen, 1993), which not only provides a framework for assessment and formulation but also governs the nature and style of therapeutic processes and relationships.

The present chapter first summarises various methods commonly deployed in systemic practice. It then offers a framework or set of themes which encompass family dynamics. Finally, it describes several applications of systems theory which have been deployed within the context of abuse work.

Methods Used in Family Work

In Chapter 7, the components or constructs that family therapists deploy towards an understanding of family dynamics were highlighted, namely: hierarchy and boundaries, role flexibility, congruent communication, goodness of fit and differentiation. Both the relevance of the constructs and the way in which they influence a family's functioning and the well-being of its members, are fundamental elements of assessment.

In assessing family dynamics, it is important to acknowledge that the families are constantly evolving. Consequently, assessment within a systemic approach is not a rigid process that has a fixed or well-defined outcome; rather, it can be seen as a fluid process which seeks to highlight the way in which constructs are working together at a given point in time. It is also therefore a continuous process, which blends in with intervention methods.

Simply stated, assessment is not distinct from intervention; both are considered part of the therapeutic process.

Methods Used in Assessment

Gilleard (1996) highlights the principal tasks for assessment and the various methods currently deployed. These are examined below.

Assessing the meaning family therapy holds for the family

Establishing the meaning therapy holds for the family is an important first step in the assessment process. While this offers the opportunity for clarifying the family's understanding of and motivation towards therapy, it is also a powerful way of addressing issues of personal responsibility, expectations and commitment towards the therapeutic context. A way of eliciting meaning is through the use of open and closed questioning.

Open questioning reflects a broad question relating to a particular area or set of circumstances: for example, 'What are your reasons for seeking help at the present time?' An open question of this type allows for a range of responses by family members and may help to ascertain the extent to which members are focused or clear in their understanding and expectations of therapy. Conversely, closed questioning is directed at a specific issue and hence allows for a more narrowed focus on particular themes: for example 'What do you fear most about coming into therapy?'

Identifying the Problem
The major objective in systemic therapy is to assist the family in identifying or reframing their 'problem' in such a way as to make it workable. As Gilleard points out, 'there is never a single problem for the family, only versions of the same one expressed in different ways'.

The main issue here is that what the family might perceive as their problem may in fact be either an expression or symptom of an underlying problem or, indeed, their solution to that problem. For example, the family may present their problem as relating to their mother's willingness to be fed by a family member. In systemic terms, however, the problem as presented by the family could be seen as a symptom of the family's long-standing difficulties in delegating roles and responsibilities to each other at a time when their normal routine is being challenged by new demands.

Methods used to assist the family in reframing itself in workable terms include circular questioning, for example asking one member of the family what another member would have said or done in response to a particular circumstance, and the reflective team, for example where the therapist may discuss or reflect openly with another therapist their views or opinions concerning aspects of family functioning as a way of enabling the family to consider alternative issues.

Of major importance in this phase is that the problem, however redefined, is seen by the family as being their problem: that is, that all family members claim responsibility in the development and resolution of their problem.

Past history and future possibilities
System theory sees families as being 'connected' in a multigenerational way where cultural, social and psychological influences permeate down from one generation to another and across generations. In this way, the problem is seen as a product of history as well as relating to current circumstances. Understanding how such influences evolve through successive transitions that families go through can help to identify recurrent themes (such as patterns of abusive behaviour, passivity or distance between family members and agenda issues). Exploring the family history in this way offers a number of opportunities for development.

Firstly, there is the opportunity to reframe responsibility for certain actions. For example, a family member may carry a disproportionate degree of responsibility and guilt for the family's problem. An exploration of the family history might suggest that blaming is a common theme running throughout generations, directed particularly at female members. In this way, the family could be seen as scapegoating that individual, which may then serve to refocus the responsibility upon the whole family.

Secondly and related to the above, there is the opportunity to understand generational expectations and boundaries. For example, the family may attribute conflicts between an adult child and their dependent parents as relating to a personality clash as a result of cohabitation. However, the family's history might suggest that conflicts have always arisen during similar circumstances in the past. The problem may then be reframed as an issue of filial obligation to care, in that boundaries, expectations, ways of operating and so on, have not been adequately resolved throughout the generations.

Thirdly, there is the opportunity to explore the family's ability to seek help during times of crisis and to draw positive meaning from their experiences. A family's ability to be open in receiving help is an important issue within the therapeutic context and is likely to reflect a common theme throughout that family's history. For example, a family member may be presenting as depressed. This is seen by the family as a consequence of a recent bereavement. However, the 'problem' may be reframed as an expression or symptom of that family's inability to gain access to wider, outside support for their bereavement. In this way, one member is seen as carrying the bereavement for all the family. This action constitutes a way of colluding with the family's need to remain closed. The issue of collusion could then provide a focus for intervention.

Two methods for exploring family history are denoted by Gilleard: a life-event calendar and a genogram. A life-event calendar involves different members of the family writing down the various transitions the family has undergone and the meaning each transition or event holds for them. This is useful in both clarifying each member's experience and highlighting what therapists term 'unpaid debts and obligations': that is, what they may have intended to say or do but did not. This experience affords the family the opportunity to reframe the current difficulties and explore ways in which they might address them.

The genogram is a type of flow chart or family tree where members of the family are described and linked in a generational pattern. The value of a genogram lies in its flexibility to explore relational issues and recurrent themes including the identification of subsystems within the family which are set apart from other subsystems by, as Gilleard suggests, rules, myths or family secrets.

Family Structure and Boundaries
As families develop throughout their life cycle, there is a continued need to redefine and renegotiate boundaries. As mentioned earlier, boundaries help to differentiate relationships between family members and serve to protect those relationships. Where boundaries become diffused, this can lead to enmeshment of roles, responsibilities and individual identities that can lead to a major source of conflict and distress for the family. A case in point is where the normal adult child–parent boundaries can become distorted when the parent is dependent upon their child for care and

support. In this example, boundaries pertaining to status, personal care and emotional support can become enmeshed between the two parties.

The opportunity for exploring changes in or violations to boundaries, examining the impact this has had for family members and ascertaining ways in which boundaries can be renegotiated are important aspects of intervention. Methods for mediating this process can include the use of a life-event calendar, a genogram or, more directly, open communication between family members.

Communication
Communication in whatever form is both a central and a crucial function of families. It acts as a mechanism for negotiation, for highlighting need, for expressing intimacy and value, and for establishing identity and control. Communication can also be mediated by what is not said or not done. Difficulties in communication, or what therapists term 'incongruent communication' can themselves be a central issue underpinning a family's problem. The way in which families communicate, the extent to which that communication is meaningful to family members, what is being communicated and what is not are central to the assessment process.

Communicative style is a product of both the family's history and current circumstances where the latter, particularly with respect to older adults, can become affected as a result of sensory loss or damage to the central and peripheral nervous system, for example as a result of stroke or dementia. Assessing communicative style can often be a complicated process and as such, it is often useful to use video recording, which allows the opportunity to reflect upon communication processes that have taken place within the session.

Indices used to understand communication include the degree of openness, honesty, variability (for example, the spread of emotions expressed), intonation and nature (instructional, informational, need-related, expression of value, controlling and so on). The therapeutic focus is expressed as the process through which family members develop congruous communication: that is, communication that is open and understood by all members in terms of its intention.

Family Dynamics
According to Gilleard, the principal task of family therapy is often considered to be 'discovering the hidden dynamic that is creating, maintaining or intensifying the family's difficulties'. The term 'dynamic' has particular relevance in systemic terms, in that it does not presuppose a single factor or issue which underlies the family's difficulties, as may be apparent in other models. Rather, the dynamic is a working hypothesis concerning several factors born from the assessment process, which work together in a fluid way.

Systemic approaches see such factors as operating in a 'circulinear' way: that is, each factor influences and is influenced by associated factors. For example, rather than saying a specific belief is directly related to a course of action, as in a purely cognitive approach, a systemic view would attempt to understand the relationship these two aspects have with each other within the framework of other influential factors. In this way, the dynamic or working hypothesis can be likened to an ecological system, for example to a fishpond where, in order to understand why the fish may be dying, one would need to understand the way in which all living organisms within the pond, the water itself, the situation of the pond within the garden, the weather conditions and so on, all interact.

Perhaps the main difference between family therapy and the fish pond analogy is that, in family therapy, the assessment process itself can perform a therapeutic function. 'Hypothesising' is the term given to the process of reflecting back to the family the hypothesis or formulation of the problem.

Methods Used in the Therapeutic Process (Neidhardt & Allen, 1993)

While many of the methods used in assessment are in themselves therapeutic, in that they contribute to the process of change, there are a number of additional methods used to address specific issues arising during therapeutic discourse. It is important to note that such methods are intended to help the family members address their problems in a manner that is relevant and meaningful for themselves. The extent to which such methods are helpful or 'effective' is demonstrated by each individual case and cannot be generalised to all family circumstances.

Joining

It is important, in terms of engaging the family, that members feel both understood and secure in the knowledge that the therapist is working on their behalf. Joining is the term given to the means by which this objective is met and involves conveying messages that the therapist is listening, empathic and concerned.

Positive Connotation

At times, family members may construe their behaviour in a negative way. Positive connotation refers to the reframing of that behaviour in positive terms. For example, an individual might see their relative's verbal outbursts towards them as an example of rejection. A positive connotation would be to suggest that the behaviour might have been a way of attempting to stop an escalation of conflict, rather than communicating rejection.

Paradoxical Messages

A paradoxical message is a form of communication (usually verbal) which is aimed at helping the family challenge or explore their beliefs or attitudes surrounding a particular issue and which may therefore help them to reframe their view of the problem. It can also serve as a powerful way of engaging the family in open communication or of eliciting emotional exchanges. The message is paradoxical in that, although it may seem deliberately contradictory or absurd in terms of its relevance to the situation, it may nevertheless generate a positive response by the family. The following example illustrates this method.

Phillip is an 85-year-old man who is incontinent of urine and being cared for by his son and daughter-in-law. When Phillip is incontinent in the lounge, his son will become verbally abusive towards him. The paradoxical message could be 'Perhaps Phillip does this to stop you both having sex.'

Whilst this sounds absurd, it may have the effect of helping the family explore their beliefs concerning the extent to which Phillip's incontinence is premeditated. Such beliefs may reflect a wider difficulty the family is having in adjusting to changes in boundaries and role expectations, which can then become a focus of address.

Provision of Information or Advice
The occurrence of abusive behaviour may be considered as reflecting an inability of family members to generate alternative ways of addressing situational tasks or conflicts. This scenario may have arisen as a product of coping mechanisms or interactional styles being passed down from one generation to another, or may simply reflect a lack of relevant knowledge surrounding another family member's difficulties or illness. As a consequence, family members may become 'locked into' a way of addressing their difficulties, particularly if such mechanisms prove effective in meeting their objectives.

Therapists may therefore seek to provide relevant information or to explore with the family a range of possible alternative, non-abusive courses of action which could be acceptable in meeting their desired objectives. The central aim of this intervention is to help family members to generate for themselves acceptable alternatives, as opposed to advising them directly to undertake changes to their behaviour.

For example, a family member suffering with dementia is likely to display some difficulty in managing their personal hygiene. The caregiver, not fully appreciating the nature of memory loss as a product of the condition, may seek to adopt punitive and unproductive learning strategies with their dependant in an attempt to help them re-establish independent functioning. Providing accurate and meaningful information to the caregiver concerning how memory is affected in dementia, and what to expect, could assist the caregiver in generating a positive approach to helping their dependant.

Encouraging Changes in Communication Styles
As mentioned previously, communication is both a crucial and a central function of families where the therapeutic focus is on helping family members develop a communicative style that is both open and understood by all family members. Achieving this objective may in part occur as a product of, for example, circular questioning, positive connotation or reviewing video recordings of sessions. The objective

may also be achieved, in part, by employing more specific methods, such as role-playing, communication sessions between family members, exploring alternative approaches, and deploying or coaching different modes of communication, for example focusing upon body language or the use of picture cards and cues.

It is important to acknowledge, however, that incongruous communication may reflect a variety of underlying dynamics which may require address before more pragmatic approaches can be deployed and accepted by family members.

Contextual Issues in Family Work

In applying systems theory to family work with older adults, Cobe (1985) highlights four main themes or directions, which may be helpful in acting as a framework for family intervention.

Independence and Dependence

In the life cycle of the family, there are continuous exchanges of goods, services and emotional caring which influence an individual's progression back and forth along the independence–dependency continuum. It is important, therefore, that the expectations of each family member match the expectations of others and that the family remains responsive to the changing capacity of its members. However, there are circumstances where the expectations of individuals are unmatched or even resisted and where abusive behaviour serves as a mechanism for reinforcing traditional boundaries, maintaining status and power, and enforcing access to goods or services or emotional gratification from an individual member where these would ordinarily be unavailable, inappropriate or simply not offered. Consider the following example.

A mother prior to her stroke held the primary status within her family. She was well respected by other family members and had a major role in offering practical and emotional support to her children. She also had a considerable degree of power over their marital relationships. Since her stroke, the mother has become wholly dependent upon her children and grandchildren for her care. She is unable to communicate effectively with them and has become ineffectual in controlling their relationships. Feeling displaced and at times ignored, she has taken to shouting and hitting out as a means of gaining recognition and asserting her status within the family system.

Affectional and Instrumental Exchanges

Affectional exchanges encompass those which meet individuals' needs for emotional security, emotional support or self-affirmation. Instrumental exchanges reflect the provision of goods, services and finances which meet an individual's more pragmatic needs. Families may change roles in respect of the provision of instrumental tasks (as in the case an older spouse who, as a result of a stroke, may no longer be able to do shopping, gardening, housework and so on), but affectional changes should remain fundamental to their relationship.

In cases where the provision of instrumental exchanges becomes problematic (for example where the caregiver has not the capacity or ability to address such tasks on behalf of their dependant), or where affectional exchanges are no longer available (as where an individual no longer recognises the other members of their family because of increasing memory difficulties), the resulting stress or emotional longing can often dissipate into abuse which serves as a mechanism for the communication of need, displacement of anger or the protection of other family members.

Filial Crisis

This reflects the change in the locus of parent–child relationships where parents can no longer be the source of support for the child in terms of meeting their personal, emotional or economic needs, but may look to the child for this. The transition is likely to promote a major challenge to both child and parent in terms of the way in which the relationship is construed, the boundaries that traditionally protect the relationship, the role requirement necessitated as a result and the nature of what is expected from the relationship in terms of emotional and practical gain. This major challenge may often precipitate a crisis in one or more members of the family, particularly where the previous relationship may itself have been difficult or where the wider social or cultural norms and expectations may significantly influence the transition.

The crisis is seen to be resolved when the transition is accomplished successfully in terms of individuals being able to accept what is possible and not possible, having had the opportunity to grieve for relevant losses to the relationship, address unresolved conflicts, establish a framework for the provision of affectional and instrumental exchanges without recourse to abuse and being able to operate comfortably within their social and cultural context.

Empowering the Family
Many families, confronted by the overwhelming stress of transitional demands, are likely to present with feelings of hopelessness, helplessness and a sense of failure. They may also have experienced difficulties in previous encounters with the helping professions. Consequently, they may present as being both defensive and resentful. This is likely to complicate the extent to which a family may be willing and able to access treatment for themselves particularly if the family is characteristically 'closed'.

It is important therefore, in the initial stages of contact, that these issues, if apparent, are acknowledged and respected and that the families are afforded the opportunity to discuss how such issues might be resolved. It is also important that families have a clear understanding of therapeutic expectations, that they are informed as to the nature and purpose of therapeutic interventions and that agreement to intervene is reached by all members of the family. A client's right to refuse therapy without prejudice should be respected at all times.

Applying Systemic Approaches to the Family Context
Systemic approaches applied to family work vary from one context to another in terms of their theoretical framework, the nature and scope of interventions deployed, the nature of the relationship between the therapist and the family, and the ability of the family themselves to make positive use of such interventions.

A further factor influencing treatment relates to the tension that often exists between the immediate need to protect the victim from further abusive acts and the family's need for long-term help and support. Where the cessation of abuse can be achieved in the short term by the family themselves, it is likely that a more protracted, long-term therapeutic approach is possible since the therapeutic relationship is unlikely to be influenced by the adverse consequences of enforced removal of the victim or perpetrator. In cases where, for whatever reason, enforced action is necessitated, this may have the effect of causing irreversible changes to both individuals and the family as a whole, the nature of which may preclude further therapeutic liaison. In such cases, removal should be established on the basis of informed consent by all family members, with both the reasons for removal and the duration of removal being properly established.

In terms of the application of systemic models, Rathbone-McCuan & Voyles (1982) highlight three models which have been used in enabling families to overcome their recourse to abusive strategies.

Contextual Family Therapy Model (Boszormenyi-Nagy & Ulrich, 1980) This model offers a long-term approach to the treatment of multigenerational families where personal and, often, emotional conflicts are associated with the victimisation of an elder.

Conflicts which give rise to abuse are considered as underlying three principal mechanisms: firstly, as a product of previously discordant multigenerational family relationships where repressed feelings of anger are expressed as vengeance, often arising during inverse family transitions, for example where the adult child, formerly dominated and possibly abused by their parent, is now responsible for the care of that parent and who therefore holds the balance of power in the relationship; secondly, where issues of filial obligation may give rise to extreme dissonance between the obligation to care for oneself or others and the obligation to care for a dependent relative; and thirdly, where abusive acts are seen as a way of addressing unmet needs. For example, the illegal accessing of a dependant's finances may also be seen as a symbolic gesture on behalf of the perpetrator which meets a need in them to feel valued or loved where that need cannot be met directly during the normal discourse of the relationship: 'If I can't have their love, I'll take their money!'

Treatment methods are usually, but not exclusively, psychodynamic in nature, involving the free expression of feelings, the addressing of unresolved conflicts and the development of alternative and productive strategies for meeting needs.

Problem-Centred Systems Family Therapy (Epstein & Bishop, 1981)
This approach seeks to identify and treat problems that arise during periods of transition which are specifically related to the process of family interactions. Problems are seen either as instrumental; that is reflecting the way in which families relate or operate with each other in terms of communicative style, role differentiation, adherence to boundaries or resolution of conflict, or as affective, reflecting the emotional experiences of family members in terms of guilt, anger, rejection or warmth. Intrapsychic issues may be acknowledged, but not seen as the central issue in underpinning abuse. Rather, that abuse is a particular manifestation of instrumental or affectional processes which have normally been passed down through the generations.

Intervention methods are varied according to what the therapist considers to be first-order or second-order changes. First-order changes involve direct interventions which have as a primary purpose the solution of an immediate problem and to decrease levels of stress; second-order changes usually involve indirect interventions to help the family change the general direction of their lives in the long term.

Where this approach is aimed at addressing the short-term cessation of abuse, or as a form of crisis intervention, the authors advocate a four-stage intervention programme.

Assessment Stage
This involves addressing the families' expectations of therapy, obtaining information regarding family structures, instrumental and affectional processes, identifying and reaching agreement regarding the target problem and relating it in functional terms.

Contracting Stage
The contracting stage involves informing the family as to the purpose and nature of therapeutic contracting, outlining options for intervention, negotiating expectations and developing the contract.

Treatment Stage
Interventions are selected on the basis of a problem-solving approach involving identifying goals, brainstorming solutions, selecting those solutions most appropriate to meeting goals, clarifying priorities, setting tasks, implementing tasks and evaluating outcomes.

Closure Stage
This stage involves summarising interventions and outcomes, establishing long-term goals and follow-up arrangements. The programme is usually implemented over six to twelve sessions.

Task-centred Model (Reid & Epstein, 1972)
Whereas the problem-centred approach identifies and intervenes with problems pertaining to relational dynamics, the task-centred approach deals with the more pragmatic issues faced by families in their attempts to deal with formal organisations, role performance, social transitions, reactive emotional distress and inadequate income. Abusive behaviour is considered neither as a product of intrapsychic conflicts (contextual family therapy model), nor as a function of intra-family dynamics (problem-centred model) but, rather, as a maladaptive coping style deployed by individual family members in achieving their defined goals.

The emphasis of the approach is therefore on the training of appropriate coping mechanisms which facilitate task completion. Intervention protocol is similar to that deployed by the problem-centred approach, although the methods used for task completion are usually behaviourally based. They include problem exploration, task selection and planning, task review, rehearsals for task outcomes or behavioural simulation, anticipation of obstacles and contingency planning. They also include procurement of concrete resources, development of reinforcing activities, direction and advice from the therapist, enhancing awareness of a client's action upon others and obtaining supportive co-operation from significant others or outside agencies.

Exercise 9.1

The Williams family live together in a four-bedroomed home situated in a multiracial area of a large city. Melvin Williams aged 75, is the father of Maurice. Maurice is 45 and runs his own electrical business. He is married to Anita, who is 43 years old and is a nurse at the local general hospital. The couple have two children, Melvin and Justine, both of whom live with their parents and have careers in the commercial sector.

Melvin came to England from Jamaica in 1948 with his wife, Clarissa. He undertook manual work at a large car factory. The couple had their son, Maurice, in 1950, but lost a second child (Louis) two years later. Three years ago, Melvin suffered a major stroke which caused paralysis of his right side, with an accompanying expressive dysphasia. Clarissa undertook to care for her husband, but died suddenly a year ago following a heart attack, whereupon Melvin moved in with his son and daughter-in-law.

Since this time, Melvin has become progressively confused, withdrawn and doubly incontinent. The bulk of his care is provided by Anita, who is finding the demands of both her job and the caregiving role extremely stressful. Maurice and Anita have drifted apart in their relationship and frequent arguments have occurred between all family members. Melvin received some regular respite care, and on one visit to your unit, bruising was noted on his upper arms, with a large swelling of his left ear. Maurice was asked how this came about and he reported that his father had fallen while he was being toileted.

On the last visit, similar injuries were observed and, in addition, it was apparent that Melvin had lost weight and was somewhat dehydrated. Abuse was suspected and a case conference was eventually held with all members of the family to discuss the family's circumstances. Initially, the family disclosed the enormous pressures they were under and agreed that Melvin should prolong the period of respite so that his physical problems could be addressed; but, in addition, they expressed their wish to continue to care for him at home.

A further meeting was held with the family, where Maurice disclosed that he had assaulted his father on several occasions. As a result of this meeting, the family agreed to accept help for themselves.

1   What would you see as being the important cultural issues you would need to consider in engaging this case and in what way would they be influential in determining how you would proceed?
2   What would you consider to be the main transitions family members are currently experiencing and are these life cycle changes likely to be congruent or dissonant?
3   Who are the main client groups involved in this case?
4   What would you consider to be the most appropriate type or types of intervention necessary in helping this family?
5   How would you go about planning intervention and which professionals or agencies would you see as important to become involved in the case?

Key Points
1   Families are dynamic systems characterised by a continuous style involving circular relationships.
2   Families are influenced by multiple transitions throughout the life cycle. The family's life cycle change may at times be congruent with those of its individual members and at other times dissonant.
3   Families are both influenced by and dependent upon the culture in which they operate and survive.
4   As a framework for understanding family dynamics, four main themes are highlighted:

   •   the continuum of independence–dependency, which characterises the nature of transitions and expectations amongst family members;
   •   affectional and instrumental exchanges which characterise the way in which family members support each other and develop a meaningful bond;

- filial crisis, which highlights the nature of particular conflicts among family members during transitions;
- empowerment, which highlights the need of families to control and influence their development.

5   Factors influencing treatment interventions include the following:

- the nature of therapist–client relationships;
- the ability of the family in making positive use of treatment;
- the tension that may arise between the need to protect the abused individual and the incorporation of abuse as the fundamental element in therapy.

6   Three main intervention models are highlighted:

- contextual family therapy, which provides a long-term psychotherapeutically oriented approach to assisting families where abuse is seen as a product of intrapsychic conflicts within family members;
- problem-centred systems family therapy, which provides a short-term systems-orientated approach to assisting families where abuse is seen as a product of instrumental or affectional processes passed down through the generations;
- task-centred approach, which provides a short-term problem-solving approach where abuse is seen as a maladaptive coping mechanism in family members endeavouring to address the more pragmatic problems faced when dealing with formal organisations, role performance, social transitions, reactive emotional distress and inadequate incomes.

Suggested Further Reading
Barusch AS, 1991, *Elder Care, Family Training and Support*, Sage, London.
Boyd-Franklin N, 1988, *Black Families In Therapy – A Multisystems Approach*, Guildford Press, London.

Falicon CJ, 1988, *Family Transitions – Continuity And Change Over The Life Cycle*, Guildford Press, London.

Froggatt A., 1990, *Family Work With Elderly People*, Macmillan, Basingstoke.

Gelles RJ & Losek DR, 1993, *Current Controversies On Family Violence*, Sage, Thousand Oaks.

Kane RA & Penrod JD, 1995, *Family Caregiving in an Ageing Society – Policy Perspectives*, Sage, London.

Neidhardt ER & Allen JA, 1993, *Family Therapy With The Elderly*, Sage, Thousand Oaks.

Pinkston EM, 1984, *Care Of The Elderly – A Family Approach*, Pergamon, Oxford.

Smith GC, Tobin SS, Robertson-Tchabo EA & Power PW, 1995, *Strengthening Ageing Families*, Sage, Thousand Oaks.

CHAPTER 10

Working with Individuals who Experience Abuse

Introduction

While the majority of abuse work is likely to focus primarily upon the family system, there are circumstances which will necessitate direct work with the victim over and above that which simply secures their protection. Victim-centred therapeutic intervention should be considered where (a) the impact of abuse is of a level and severity which warrants direct intervention, (b) where the client's ability to partake in or tolerate wider systemic interventions is restricted by virtue of psychological, physical or sociocultural influences, or (c) where the client seeks to receive treatment independently.

In working with victims, there are likely to be three major issues which will influence the course and outcome of therapy.

The Nature and Severity of the Abusive Experience

This relates to the impact of abuse upon a client's physical, psychological and social functioning, which is described in detail in Chapter 5. Inasmuch as abuse can give rise to discrete pathologies, such as depression, post-traumatic stress disorder, physical illness or disability; in reality, a client is likely to present with a configuration of difficulties which may necessitate multimodal or multiprofessional intervention. Priority will therefore need to be given according to the type of intervention that is appropriate at any given point in time. For example, medical needs might take priority over psychological needs or, where a client is severely depressed, their illness will need treatment before they are likely to benefit from a purely psychological approach.

The Client's Personal Capacity to Influence Change

Essentially, this refers to the client's physical and psychological qualities which they 'bring into' the therapeutic context and which may influence outcome. Factors include their physical propensity in being able to communicate or to exert behavioural coping mechanisms, their cognitive ability relating to insight and planning and problem solving, the extent to which they may hold fixed or rigid belief systems concerning themselves, their current social circumstances and the degree of openness they are able to afford in self-disclosure and emotional expression.

In many circumstances, a great deal of preparatory work may need to be carried out before the commencement of direct treatment relating to the abuse.

The Extent to Which the Client Environment has the Potential for Supporting Positive Change

The term 'environment' relates to both social and material factors which may influence a client's ability to effect and maintain positive change. At a micro level, reference is made to such factors as the living environment, in terms of the availability and access a client might have to 'safe' areas for the purposes of escape or privacy; the nature, magnitude and distribution of power held by various members within the family system, the availability of social and practical support both on a continuing basis and at times of crisis; and the extent to which the client is dependent upon others for their personal well-being.

At a macro level, reference is made to the wider ageist variables which may operate against the client making positive progress in terms of wider community acknowledgement and support. In addition, availability and access to valued life experience and the extent to which the client is able to gain the appropriate support necessary if requiring recourse to legal procedures. The present chapter discusses, in broad terms, the nature of therapeutic interventions, and highlights the specific methods which can be used where the client is experiencing confusion or memory loss.

The Nature of Therapeutic Interventions

Therapeutic intervention in abuse work is usually directed towards a number of principal foci or tasks.

Development of a Therapeutic Relationship with a Client which Fosters a Culture of Trust, Openness and Security

In meeting this objective, it is important that the therapist or helper is non-judgemental in their responses to the client; that they are able to listen, acknowledge and afford sufficient space for the client in their self-disclosures and expression of feelings; that they promote feelings of empathy and value; and that issues pertaining to the boundaries of confidentiality and disclosure are properly explained to the client.

Helping the Client to Overcome Distress and Emotional Blocks

The emotional consequences of abuse are likely to be varied in terms both of nature and severity. Many therapists believe that, in order for the individual to begin to address the various cognitive and behavioural changes necessary for their development, the emotional overlay caused by their experiences will need to be expressed and worked through. A method which is shown to be particularly useful in clients experiencing some form of acute stress reaction is known as traumatic incident reduction. This method (often included in psychological debriefing programmes) involves breaking up the incident into various segments, asking the client to relive the segment covertly, then asking them to disclose their images and emotions surrounding that segment.

This process is rehearsed several times and over successive segments until such time as feelings and images of the incident are no longer distressing or intrusive. This is achieved as a product of desensitisation to thoughts or images which elicit fear or anxiety reactions.

A second approach, commonly used where clients may construe the abuse as being legitimate, is to challenge their views directly and to help the client explore and express their feelings freely. The belief that an act of abuse has some legitimacy is often a product of long-term discrimination and disempowerment: for example, where a client has been in a relationship where they have been encouraged to play a subservient role, or where they have been pressured to accept the blame for difficulties that have arisen within the relationship.

Techniques which may be helpful include the use of visual imagery, such as creating an internal image of the perpetrator and asking the client to direct their emotions towards that image. Letter writing can also be used, for example, a client can be encouraged to commit their feelings to paper, as if they were writing to the perpetrator. It may also be possible to facilitate direct confrontation with the perpetrator, with a third party to oversee and help control proceedings.

Apart from assisting the client in emotional expression, this approach has the added advantage of empowering the client at a conceptual and emotional level over the perpetrator. Disempowerment, leading to poor self-esteem, internalisation of anger and social withdrawal, is common following abusive acts.

Assisting the Client in their Personal and Social Development
This entails the development of appropriate cognitive and behavioural strategies, which enable the client to exert control and influence over their lives and those to whom they relate. It also enables them to develop a sense of self-worth and to support a life style for themselves, which promotes self-care and positive meaning. Meeting these objectives is achieved through a combination of the various modes of treatment deployed, the benefits achieved as a result of the therapeutic relationship itself and the value of additional support services which may be available.

Decisions concerning which particular type or combination of therapeutic interventions would be most appropriate for the client should ideally be focused upon a thorough assessment of the factors indicated in Chapter 6. Thus, for some clients inexperienced in social confrontation, an assertiveness programme may be all that is needed, whereas for those clients experiencing a diminished view of themselves and who may lack self-confidence as a result of many years of abuse or oppression, recourse to protracted psychotherapy may be necessary. Consider the following example.

Mr and Mrs Stewart had been married for about 50 years. They were in their early seventies and both were rather frail owing to a combination of illnesses. They had one son and three grandchildren. About two years previously, their son had become separated from his family and had started to drink heavily. The circumstances had caused the couple much distress and, a year after their son's separation from his wife, Mr Stewart unfortunately died following a massive heart attack. Given Mrs Stewart's frailty and the fact that her son was now living alone, she decided to sell her house and move in with him.

The relationship proved disastrous, as her son began to increase his drinking and became dependent upon his mother for financial assistance. At times, when she declined to give him money, her resistance was met with both physical and verbal abuse. Mrs Stewart became more withdrawn, declining social contacts with her friends and eventually becoming depressed, which led to a hospital admission. Following a number of weeks of intensive psychiatric care, Mrs Stewart was referred to Psychology Services for treatment as an in-patient. At the first assessment, Mrs Stewart appeared withdrawn and very tearful, and held a very diminished view of herself and her future. Nevertheless, she was able to express her difficulties in some depth.

Initially, a cognitive therapy approach was undertaken which focused upon her belief systems surrounding her involvement in precipitating her son's abusive acts. Through a process of helping the client rethink or 'reframe' her relationship with her son, she was able to relocate responsibility for the abuse from herself to her son. This was followed by a number of sessions devoted primarily to psychological debriefing which focused upon a number of specific instances of abuse which were particularly devastating for her. After about six sessions, Mrs Stewart decided to confront her son directly by writing a letter in which she was able to express both her anger and her sadness at the circumstances which had prevailed and in addition to express her hopes and fears for the future. The following sessions were devoted primarily to the loss of her husband. The final session explored her own needs and those important life experiences which would assist in developing meaning and motivation in her life.

> As a result of treatment, the client decided to move into warden-controlled accommodation and subsequent follow-up sessions suggested that she had developed a number of close relationships with others and in addition was able to re-establish her relationship with her son.

The above example illustrates therapeutic intervention for those clients who have the ability to engage this style of therapy. However, there are other clients, particularly those experiencing confusion, who may be less able to contribute or make use of an intensive insight-oriented approach but whose need to resolve feelings and conflicts incurred as a result of abuse are nevertheless the same.

Working with Confused People

It is often the case that people suffering from confusion are construed as totally unable to benefit from counselling-based approaches. Such conceptions are unfounded. Firstly, research shows that many individuals, particularly those in the early stages of dementia, are able to register and recall significantly meaningful recent life events; secondly, the sufferer's behaviour is not simply a product of random events that occur within the brain: rather, what professionals term 'confusion' is a product of an individual's attempt to make sense of their experiences (Harding & Palfrey, 1997).

It is therefore inappropriate to believe that the client-centred methods cannot be used effectively with this client group. What are required are ways of deploying such procedures in a manner that considers the limitations of the client but which enhances their available strengths. Furthermore, whereas the basis of therapy in non-confused clients assumes that the client will build upon therapeutic gains in the long term, in dementia sufferers therapeutic gain is more appropriately focused on the resolution of distress or conflict in the short term.

In helping such clients overcome the psychological impact of abuse, a number of therapeutic interventions may be helpful.

Validation Therapy (Feil, 1982)

Basically, validation therapy assumes that many adults are, for various reasons, unable to resolve their conflicts, which leads to despair, isolation and discontent. They withdraw from present reality, which has no meaning for them, and create a fantasy existence through which emotional and inner conflicts can be expressed. Through the use of client-centred interactions (reflection, exploration, self-awareness and so on) individuals are encouraged to express their feelings and in so doing to assist in the resolution of conflicts.

The approach has been criticised on the basis of making unproven assumptions and being of value only to those individuals who are displaying a pseudo-dementia of emotional origin, but validation therapy may be helpful for this latter group of clients where the impact of abuse is a central causative factor in the clinical presentation.

Resolution Therapy (Goudie & Stokes, 1989)

Resolution therapy is specifically designed for use in counselling clients experiencing an organic dementia, but can also be used in cases of pseudo-dementia. The central premise in resolution therapy is that the confused behaviour represents an individual's active attempt to make sense of their experiences and to communicate their needs in the 'here and now'. Unlike validation therapy, resolution therapy makes no assumptions concerning the relationship between previous unresolved conflicts. Rather, it attempts to ascertain the functional relationship between the environmental setting, the associated behaviour and the concealed meaning underlying the behaviour in terms of current need and resulting feelings. Table 10.1 illustrates this relationship.

The emphasis of resolution therapy is on seeking to understand the concealed meaning of a person's behaviour and to acknowledge their feelings as currently expressed. Therapeutic intervention seeks to develop ways to assist the individual in meeting their needs and overcoming distressing emotions. Interventions may therefore include skills of reflective listening and exploration, the provision of warmth and empathy in association with wider initiatives involving modifications to the environment, home support, respite care and work with the family or carer–dependant relationship.

Table 10.1 *Example Of Resolution Therapy Formulation*

Setting	Confused message/ Behaviour	Concealed meaning	Underlying feelings
Primary care giver hits elderly confused man after he urinates on the floor	'Why have I been hit?' 'What have I done wrong?' Individual then starts to wander around the house, calling out.	'I need to feel secure.' 'I need to understand Why this is happening to me?' 'I need to be comforted.'	Fear, insecurity, pain, anxiety

Life Review Counselling/Reminiscence Therapy (Butler, 1963)
This approach has been traditionally used to help clients restore continuity and meaning to their lives and to work through unresolved conflicts experienced at different points in their life cycle. The approach has similarities with validation therapy, but does not focus upon a client's immediate feelings. Essentially, the process involves rediscovering significant life events, exploring the meaning or impact such events held for the individual (both positive and negative), integrating life events into a meaningful whole and assisting the client in coming to terms with past regrets in the resolution of conflicts.

The application of reminiscence therapy with confused clients can be particularly useful in cases where the individual has been subjected to abuse over many years. However, research showing the effectiveness of this approach in alleviating depression amongst dementia sufferers (Goldwasser *et al*, 1987) suggests that it should be used as part of a continuous programme of care.

Group Work with Individuals

Group based interventions have several advantages over direct 'one to one' work. Firstly, while undergoing one-to-one treatment, many abused individuals may nevertheless continue to feel isolated or marginalised. Working through their difficulties with others in a similar predicament enables a sense of normalisation, a recognition that abuse is an ordinary experience of life that happens to others as well as to oneself. Secondly, the group context provides a basis for support and contribution, which enhances a sense of status, purpose and security. Finally, the very presence of many individuals provides an opportunity for problem solving and brainstorming.

In order that groups are able to function in this way it is important that group membership is of appropriate size (about six to eight is advised by social psychologists) and that individuals are both willing and able to engage the group in a productive manner. For many clients, particularly those who are psychologically extremely vulnerable, exposure to group settings may have a deleterious effect. Therefore careful assessment is required in ascertaining which clients might benefit from group work and the need for preparatory work should always be considered.

Group work can take several forms. Groups may be structured in terms of following a specific agenda or programme and involve the incorporation of the therapist or facilitator. Alternatively, groups may be unstructured (as with self-help groups) with group members free to decide their own agenda and procedures. Traditionally, open or unstructured groups involve participants who have usually undergone a degree of personal therapy or development prior to engagement.

Exercise 10.1

Ranjit Singh is a 78-year-old gentleman who is frail and requires the use of a walking frame to assist his mobility. He lives alone, but receives some support from his son, who has a drink problem.

Over a period of approximately eighteen months, Mr Singh has been physically assaulted by his son on various occasions and has had his finances misappropriated. He attends your day hospital and has given you to believe that he is being abused. However, he has declined the suggestion that you should interview his son.

---

1   What would you consider to be the main personal and cultural issues that might affect Mr Singh's ability to work with you?
2   In the light of the above, what action would you take towards assisting your client?

Exercise 10.2

Gladys is a frail 82-year old woman living in warden-controlled accommodation. Over a five-year period, she lost two sisters and her husband, for whom she continues to grieve. A niece is the only remaining relative, but she lives some 30 miles away and is only able to visit Gladys once a month. Nevertheless, Gladys has made several close friends within her locality and attends a social club once a week.

Two months ago, when Gladys was returning home from her club, she was attacked by two individuals who physically assaulted her and snatched her handbag. She received head injuries during the attack but did not receive any help until a neighbour spotted her about three hours later. She was admitted to the local general hospital for acute treatment, then transferred to a rehabilitation hospital for further care.

On admission, Gladys presented as withdrawn, mildly confused, agitated and shaky on her legs and became tearful for no apparent reason. She reported poor appetite, nightmares with difficulty in sleeping, depressed mood and said that she was experiencing recurrent thoughts and images of the incident on a daily basis.

---

1 What further investigations would you undertake to clarify the client's mental state, or to whom would you refer for such investigations?

2 What would you consider to be the client's major needs at this time and what actions would you suggest should happen in order to help Gladys meet her needs?

3 What type or types of treatment interventions would you consider to be most appropriate in this case, and at what point during the client's care do you feel this intervention should be appropriately implemented?

4 What would you consider to be the most important environmental issues which might influence Glady's ability to adjust following discharge?

Exercise 10.3

Mary is a 78-year-old woman was admitted into residential care about 18 months ago following the sudden death of her husband. She has Parkinson's Disease and is moderately confused. On admission, Mary was malnourished and exhibited the latter stages of bruising on the inner sides of her legs. Her genitalia were swollen and rather tender and she became very agitated upon examination. Since this time, Mary has been observed to become notably agitated and to have a tendency to scream out when staff attempt to toilet her. You suspect that Mary has been a victim of sexual abuse and neglect, possibly over a protracted period.

---

1 What further information would you require to support your assumption?
2 What would you consider to be Mary's main needs as regards her abusive experiences?
3 What type of approach or approaches would you consider as being helpful in assisting Mary, both at times relating to toileting and more widely?

Key Points

1 Several factors affect therapeutic processes and outcomes:
   - the nature and severity of abusive experiences,
   - the client's personal capacity to influence change,
   - the extent to which the environment has a potential for supporting positive change. This includes access to a 'safe environment', availability and extent of practical and social support, the nature of power positions help by family members, and the nature and extent of ageist practices operating within the client's local community and organisational setting.

2 Therapeutic interventions are primarily focused upon the following:
   - the development of a therapeutic relationship which fosters trust, openness, security and acceptance,

- assisting the client in emotional expression, overcoming the distress or impact caused by the abuse and addressing emotional blocks,
- assisting the client in their personal and social development.

3 Therapeutic methods include the following:
- cognitive and behavioural therapies,
- psychological debriefing/critical incident reduction,
- psychotherapy.

4 Methods involved in assisting confused clients who have been abused include the following:
- validation therapy,
- resolution therapy,
- life review counselling/reminiscence therapy.

5 Group work with individuals has certain advantages over direct one-to-one work:
- helping clients achieve a sense of normalisation,
- serving as a context for achieving wider support and affirmation,
- acting as a means of brainstorming solutions.

Suggested Further Reading

Breckman RS & Adelman RD, *1988, Strategies for Helping Victims of Elder Mistreatment,* Sage, Thousand Oaks.

Heron J, 1990, *Helping The Client – A Creative Practical Guide,* Sage, London.

Kirkwood C, 1993, *Leaving Abusive Partners: From the Scars of Survival to the Wisdom for Change,* Sage, London.

Nelson-Jones R, 1982, *The Theory and Practice of Counselling Psychology,* Holt, Rinehart & Winston.

O'Leary E, 1995, *Counselling The Older Patient,* Chapman & Hall, London.

Parkinson F, 1993, *Post-Trauma Stress,* Insight.

Resick P & Schnicke M, 1993, *Cognitive Processing Therapy For Rape Victims: A Treatment Manual,* Sage, Thousand Oaks.

Skinner EA, 1995, *Perceived Control, Motivation And Coping,* Sage, London.

CHAPTER 11

Working with People who Perpetrate Abuse

Introduction

The focus of this chapter is on working with those who perpetrate abuse to whom the victim is directly related or upon whom the victim is dependent for their care. In some cases the perpetrator may be the dependant themselves. Those who perpetrate abuse as 'outsiders' are likely to be catered for in other settings such as forensic psychiatric settings or within other professional organisations.

Although the focus of abuse work with perpetrators is usually kept within their relational or family settings, there are circumstances where individual work is appropriate either individually or as a step towards integrated therapy with the wider family system or subsystem. This is likely to be apparent in cases where it is the expressed wish of the client to seek help for themselves or where the involvement of significant others (including the victim) is not possible for whatever reason.

In addition, while the extinction of abusive behaviour will be the primary intended outcome of intervention, there may be other factors pertaining to the client's social, psychological and physical well-being that also require address as part of an integrated treatment plan.

Issues in Treatment

Clearly, one of the most important factors in influencing therapeutic processes and outcomes relates to the nature of the therapeutic relationship. In addressing abuse as the primary focus of intervention, the fact that abuse carries legal implications poses a particular challenge to this relationship, affecting the extent to which client confidentiality can be secured (Griffiths *et al*, 1993). In working with perpetrators, it is therefore advisable that the therapist, prior to commencement, (a) has a thorough understanding of their legal and contractual obligations in reporting abuse, (b) that such obligations are fully disclosed to the client when formulating therapeutic contracts, and (c) the therapist has access to appropriate supervision or support if and when contractual boundaries become threatened.

A second issue pertains to the need for openness in self-disclosure. In the same way and for the same reasons that victims may be reluctant to disclose abuse, so might perpetrators. It is important therefore that the therapist is sensitive to the possibility that their responses or behaviour towards the client may be considered judgemental.

Finally, it is worth reiterating that abuse, like any other form of behaviour, is goal-directed. Interventions aimed at simply inhibiting or preventing abuse from occurring, without developing other mechanisms for achieving the desired outcome, are unlikely to be helpful for the client or their wider relationships in the long term. Consequently, therapy should ideally be directed towards two parallel outcomes: the cessation of abusive behaviour and the strengthening of a client's personal and relational integrity.

The Nature of Therapeutic Interventions
Broadly speaking, therapeutic interventions tend to fall into two main categories: those which are goal directed and those which are process centred. Goal-specific interventions are usually designed on the basis of a functional model or working hypothesis which defines the nature and interrelationship between social, emotional, cognitive, environmental and behavioural variables in terms of their influence upon the target problem (see Figure 11.1). Treatment is planned incorporating one or more discreet types of interventions intended to effect specific outcomes. In contrast, process-centred approaches are concerned with the relational dynamics that occur between client and therapist in effecting positive change. Intervention, while largely unplanned, is nevertheless guided at various points throughout therapy in accordance with the issues that the client brings to the therapeutic context.

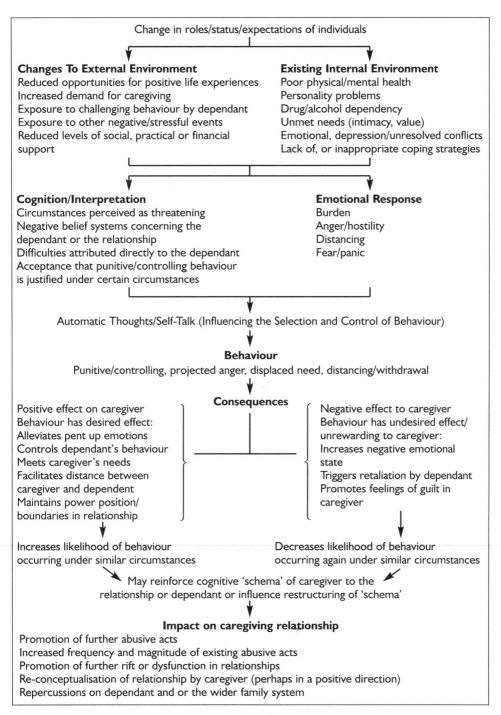

Figure 11.1 *A functional model of abuse*

The emphasis of process-centred therapy (for example, dynamic psychotherapy) lies within the process of exploration, expression of feelings, reframing and challenging in helping the client resolve emotional conflicts and in developing a meaningful and fulfilling life. For some clients, abusive behaviour may simply reflect either an absent or a maladaptive deployment of cognitive and behavioural strategies, which occur under specific conditions, such as when under extreme stress or when the behaviour of their dependant is construed as threatening.

In these cases the use of cognitive and behavioural interventions (stress management training or assertiveness training for example) as part of a wider programme may be sufficient (see Figure 11.1). In other cases however, factors which influence abusive behaviour may be more complex and reflect wider issues intrinsic to the client's ability to function both individually and within the relational context. Where this is evident, a more global approach to intervention, possibly incorporating other professional disciplines and social support structures, may be necessitated.

Given the above, a thorough assessment of the client's physical, psychological, social and environmental circumstances is required in order to ascertain both the appropriate nature and level of therapeutic intervention and the context in which it is best applied.

Finally, the most important psychological prerequisite if a client is to benefit from therapy is personal responsibility and accountability. Whatever mode of treatment may be considered appropriate for the client, it is unlikely to be beneficial or even plausible if the client does not view it as their own responsibility to change their behaviour. While external circumstances may be influential in giving rise to a client's current problems and in influencing the extent to which positive change can occur, it is the client's responsibility to effect change for themselves. The following example illustrates.

Mr and Mrs Nash are both in their seventies and have been married for about 40 years. They live in a two-bedroomed bungalow. This was Mr Nash's second marriage, having had two sons from his previous marriage. He has been suffering from a dementing illness for about eight years. Mrs Nash has been the primary caregiver for her husband, although over the past two years she has become increasingly frail herself. The couple have been in receipt of home care services for about a year.

During a recent visit to her general practitioner, Mrs Nash broke down in tears, telling her doctor that, over the past six months, she had become increasingly distressed about not being able to look after her husband appropriately. She described the mornings as particularly difficult, as they would often come to blows during Mrs Nash's attempts at dressing her husband. The doctor referred Mrs Nash to a community psychiatric nurse who undertook to provide Mrs Nash with support.

The initial session focused upon enabling Mrs Nash to express her feelings openly and to discuss in more depth her feelings about the couple's relationship and her fears for the future. Clearly, it was Mrs Nash's desire to continue to provide care for her husband, although she was in a quandary as to how she could cope with the morning episodes.

The second session entailed Mrs Nash disclosing further specific information about the couple's routine throughout the day. In particular, she was asked to keep a diary which would show the times when abusive interactions took place, circumstances immediately prior to the abuse, including her thoughts and feelings, the nature of the abuse and the circumstances immediately following the abuse, in terms of how she coped and the consequences for her husband (see the example of the ABC Diary in Chapter 7).

The diary yielded the following information. The times when Mr and Mrs Nash came to blows centred primarily around the morning routine, where Mrs Nash would wake her husband with a cup of tea and tell him that he had to get dressed in order to go to the day centre. She would then assist her husband to the bathroom, where she would wash and shave him, and then return him to the bedroom for the purpose of removing his pyjamas and then dressing him in his day clothes. It appeared that, when Mrs Nash began to remove her husband's pyjamas, he would become verbally abusive.

On occasions Mrs Nash would simply remove herself from the situation and telephone the day centre in order to inform them that her husband was unwell and would not be able to attend. On other occasions, she would persist in attempting to remove her husband's pyjamas, telling him again that he needed to go to the day centre and that she was not going to put up with his silly behaviour. On such occasions the couple's exchanges would escalate, with Mr Nash often hitting his wife and she would respond by hitting him back. Mrs Nash's abuse, while stressful to her, nevertheless enabled her to continue with dressing her husband.

The nurse asked Mrs Nash how she coped with the evening routine where abuse was obviously not apparent. Mrs Nash reported that, during the evening, her husand's sons would assist in his bedtime routine, which did not evidence any difficulty. Following a review of the information, a problem formulation was developed between the nurse and Mrs Nash which yielded a functional pattern. Firstly, it was suggested to Mrs Nash that her husband was likely to be particularly confused following a period of sleep. Therefore, in the first instance, she could perhaps slowly awaken her husband with his cup of tea, and introduce herself as his wife, gradually orienting him to the fact that it was morning.

Secondly, it was unlikely that Mr Nash would make any sense of the notion that he had to attend a day centre. It was therefore suggested that Mrs Nash introduce the daily routine by associating it with a similar routine in Mr Nash's past which was likely to be more meaningful such as times when he would need to go to work.

Thirdly, it was pointed out to Mrs Nash that, given her husband's state of confusion, he would most probably misconstrue his wife's objectives, in that, as far as he was concerned, a strange lady had come into his bedroom and attempted to remove his clothes. Understandably, Mr Nash was likely to become resistive as he construed this intervention as threatening. It was also pointed out that in Mr Nash's past, he would dress himself, not in the bedroom, but in the bathroom. It was therefore suggested that Mrs Nash should not remove her husband from the bathroom following his shave but, rather, provide him with each article of his clothing in the appropriate sequence, which would allow him to dress himself.

Finally, in the event that Mr Nash started to become agitated or verbally abusive, it was suggested that Mrs Nash should temporarily leave the room, returning about 10 minutes later, by which time Mr Nash was likely to have settled. In functional terms, there were a number of antecedents identified which, taken together, increased the risk of abusive behaviour occurring: the level of confusion Mr Nash was experiencing at this time in the morning, the fact that he was unlikely to recognise his wife, and that he always had been a rather independent and reserved individual who never took kindly to being cared for.

In addition, Mrs Nash was also highly stressed and appeared to rehearse various forms of negative 'self talk', which further accentuated her stress prior to undressing her husband. Furthermore, her communicative style was in any event rather challenging and not particularly meaningful to her husband. The reinforcing consequences, which increased the likelihood of Mrs Nash continuing to behave in an abusive manner, were related to her goal of dressing her husband, this being, on most occasions, achieved. Whilst this caused her great distress, it did enable him to attend the day centre. Finally, the reasons why difficulties were not encountered when Mr Nash's sons carried out the evening routine seemed to relate primarily to the fact that they were males and therefore seen as less threatening to her husband.

The suggested changes were rehearsed a number of times within the therapeutic context and, after a period of four sessions, were implemented by Mrs Nash during the morning scenario. Overall, this approach proved to be successful in enabling Mrs Nash to manage her husband's morning routine. A number of further sessions were devoted primarily to helping Mrs Nash to work through the various losses suffered in her marriage over the previous years, as a consequence of her husband's illness and to re-establish social relationships with her family and friends.

Exercise 11.1

Arthur is a 75-year-old man who lives with his wife Constance, who is aged 73. The couple have been married for about 30 years, both having had previous spouses. Arthur's first marriage was fraught with difficulties and he divorced his wife as a consequence of her alcoholism in 1960. Constance's first husband died suddenly in 1958 following an accident at work. Both Arthur and Constance had children from their first marriages.

The couple met at a social club in 1963 and married in 1965. The marriage proved very positive for them and they were able to develop good relationships with each other's children. About five years ago, Arthur's son Michael ran into financial difficulties with his business and Arthur agreed to pay off his son's debts. While this imposed a considerable financial strain on the couple, it was assumed that Michael would be in a position to help the couple out at a later date. Unfortunately, this help did not materialise as Michael's business went into receivership two years later. As a result, the couple decided to sell their home and move into a one-bedroomed flat. Both the change in accommodation and the couple's financial problems became a source of much tension.

Their difficulties were further compounded when Constance suffered a stroke a year later which caused her severe expressive and receptive difficulties. While her problems necessitated Arthur devoting much of his time to caring for her, the nature and level of intimacy the couple had formerly shared declined significantly.

Following a recent visit to the couple, Arthur asked if he could speak to you alone. During the interview he became very tearful and disclosed to you, indirectly at first, that he had forced himself sexually upon Constance on several occasions and that, while he felt guilty at his actions, he nevertheless believed intimacy to be important for both of them. He then went on to request help in dealing with the situation.

---

1   Given the above circumstances, would you consider that Arthur is abusing his wife and, if so, what would you see as being your primary obligations as a result?

2   Consider your initial feelings towards both Arthur and Constance. To what extent and in what way would you consider these to influence any further actions you would take? For example, could you work with Arthur directly and without prejudice?

3   What would you consider to be the main factors which influence Arthur's behaviour? Try and incorporate these within a functional model.

4   What further information would you require before embarking upon a therapeutic programme with Arthur?

5   What type or types of interventions would you consider which might be helpful in this case?

6   Assuming you were responsible for co-ordinating a care plan for Arthur, how would you set about achieving this in terms of objectives, required resources (social, professional and practical), procedures and contingencies?

7   What would you consider as being your own needs, if any, in undertaking to work with Arthur?

8   Assume that Arthur did not report abusing his wife but, from his report, you suspected abuse to be occurring. What action would you take and why? In addition, what would you consider to be the benefits and costs of your actions?

Key Points

1   In work with perpetrators, the therapeutic relationship is influenced by three major factors:
   • legal ramifications in influencing issues of confidentiality;
   • openness and disclosure by the client may be limited owing to their feelings of threat and guilt;
   • the continuation of abuse by the client of their dependant.

2   In working with perpetrators the therapist should ideally:
   • have a thorough understanding of their legal and contractual obligations in reporting abuse;
   • consider the difficulties the client may have in disclosing abusive acts;

157

- ensure that both the nature of interventions and desired outcomes are fully discussed with the client prior to intervention.

3   Interventions tend to fall into two main categories:
- goal-directed methods which are based upon functional assessment of the target problem and which include one or more specific types of treatments aimed at problem resolution;
- process-centred methods which focus upon the process of exploration, expression of feelings, reframing and challenging in helping the client resolve emotional conflicts and develop alternative life styles.

4   Of primary importance in therapy is the extent to which the client is able to take personal responsibility for and control over their behaviour.

Suggested Further Reading

Barusch AS, 1991, *Elder Care, Family Training and Support*, Sage, London.

Boyd-Franklin N, 1988, *Black Families In Therapy – A Multisystems Approach*. Guildford Press, London.

Falicon CJ, 1988, *Family Transitions – Continuity and Change over the Life Cycle*, Guildford Press, London.

Froggatt A, 1990, *Family Work with Elderly People*, Macmillan, Basingstoke.

Gelles RJ & Loseke DR, 1993, *Current Controversies on Family Violence*, Sage, Thousand Oaks.

Kane RA & Penrod JD, 1995, *Family Caregiving in an Ageing Society – Policy Perspectives*, Sage, Thousand Oaks.

Neidhardt ER & Allen JA, 1993, *Family Therapy with the Elderly*, Sage, Thousand Oaks.

Pinkston EM, 1984, *Care Of The Elderly – A Family Approach*, Pergamon Press, Oxford.

Smith GC, Tobin SS, Robertson-Tchabo EA & Power PW, 1995, *Strengthening Ageing Families*, Sage, Thousand Oaks.

Part 4

Abuse within Institutional and Professional Care Settings

CHAPTER 12

Professional Caregiving and the Experience of Institutional Care

Introduction

The abuse of older people in institutional settings has long been recognised, although not taken seriously until reports such as that by Robb (1967), which highlighted the considerable cruelty that occurs as a part of everyday life in these settings (Bennett & Kingston, 1993). As was recognised in Chapter 2, there is little in the way of significant statistics on the prevalence of elder abuse and neglect within these types of settings in the United Kingdom. We are therefore reliant on the statistics from the United States to indicate this. Even though the figures quoted earlier in Chapter 2 have limited transferability to the UK, they leave little doubt as to the need to investigate and respond to this issue.

The concern over abuse in institutional settings has gained greater impetus as a consequence of the increase in the number of institutional settings in the community, arising from government policies since the late 1960s. With the advent of the NHS and Community Care Act (1990) the diversity of care provided by formal caregivers has increased even further (Peace *et al*, 1997). This, coupled with the remaining provision of NHS and social services institutional care, highlights a substantive area where the quality of care provision needs to be addressed, exploring to what extent it meets client need and provides quality of life, quality of care and freedom from abuse.

Although residential establishments are subject to inspection, a number of qualitative research studies have shown consistently that abuse occurs within residential and nursing home settings in the UK (Lee Treweek, 1994; Willcocks *et al*, 1987; Counsel and Care, 1992). It could be argued that, given that the numbers of older people living in institutional settings is around 4 to 5 per cent (Bond, 1993) and therefore only a small percentage of the total older population, the number experiencing abuse will be insignificant. However, for many reasons, abuse within these settings should not be ignored. Firstly, because the older people who reside in residential care are increasingly likely to be frail physically and to have dementia and other health problems, they are more vulnerable. Secondly, and related to the first reason, due to their vulnerability, the power within these settings frequently lies with the staff, who are able to control even the smallest aspects of these residents' lives if they so wish (Willcocks *et al*, 1987). Thirdly, the UKCC (1994) report an increase in the number of complaints against nursing staff who are working with older people. For the year 1993/1994, approximately 47 per cent of complaints were about staff working with older people, compared with approximately 25 per cent in 1990/1991. Finally, as stated in Chapter 1, even one case of abuse is one too many (Phillipson, 1993a): older people have a right to expect the same standards of care that younger people would expect.

This chapter, and the next one, intend to address this issue specifically, exploring the reasons why abuse occurs, the risk factors associated with abuse in residential settings, intervention and prevention. Obviously, some of the information provided in other chapters, in particular Chapter 10, is as relevant to older people in institutional settings. However, a key difference is the nature of the relationship in which the abuse takes place – one with formal caregivers – and also of the setting, one which is now their home but also home to many other older people.

The present chapter will therefore place abuse in residential settings in context. Firstly, the reasons why residential care becomes necessary for older people are addressed, as is the significance of this for the older person. Secondly, the risk factors for abuse will be outlined and discussed, using the framework developed by Pillemer (1988) as a basis for understanding the nature of abuse in institutional settings.

The Experience of Residential Care

To gain an understanding of the significance of a move into any form of residential care for older people, one first needs to understand the meaning of home. Home conjures up many images for us as individuals, some of which will be very positive, and are likely to centre on the psychological aspects of home, such as the feeling of belonging, the relationships that exist or existed, and the sense of control over what happens within that domain. This is, if anything, likely to be more true for older people, who, in the face of other losses, view their own home as one of the few areas in their life over which they have control (Willcocks *et al*, 1987).

Willcocks *et al* indicate that the significance of home is such that thoughts of residential care are far from older people's minds. The contemplation of this form of care comes only as a last resort, and even then with considerable reluctance. Their reticence is argued to have a number of causes, one of which is succinctly outlined by Peace *et al* (1997):

> It can also be argued that the majority of older people, when they come to consider the options for coping as they become frailer in old age, continue to put aside, if not reject, the residential option. Such sidelining is not because it is a glaringly cruel institutional phenomenon; it is clearly not. We would argue that, because residential care is still perceived as a threat to the self, potential residents are compelled to resist, even when the need for the benefits and support on offer is overwhelming. Losing individuality … is not to be countenanced. (p120)

Older people are also described as fearing the labelling that comes with admission and the belief that exit from residential care comes only through death (Willcocks *et al*, 1987). Whatmore *et al* (1990) identified in their research older people's fear of loss of autonomy and independence as a consequence of their need for care. It certainly seems that this loss of individuality and self is more likely to occur in residential and nursing home care, where routines may be imposed according to the needs of the institution as a whole.

Admission to residential care is therefore often only occurring in circumstances where to remain at home would be impossible owing to extensive care needs as a result of physical and/or psychological disability and lack of significant support networks. Because of women's increased longevity and their greater experience of chronic ill health, they experience a higher risk of admission to residential care (Victor, 1991). It is widely acknowledged that the breakdown of a family's ability to give care and/or the loss of a partner within the context of the need for care also increases the risk of admission (Rankin *et al*, 1992; Victor, 1991). It can therefore be seen that the circumstances surrounding admission often involve considerable losses for the older person, which are then compounded by the loss of their home. This is further compounded by the meaning that this would have for them in terms of their links with their community, their history, their culture and their sense of self (Peace *et al*, 1997; Pietrukowicz *et al*, 1991).

Various authors suggest that the events leading up to admission to care are as likely to have a profound effect on the individual's experience of care as the institution itself (Willcocks *et al*, 1987; Peace *et al*, 1997; Norman, 1980). Wilcocks' study showed that older people often have little choice about the move into care, with the decisions being made by family or 'well-meaning professionals' who believe that the older person can no longer remain at home. The impact of this must not be understated, many older people enter care with feelings of disempowerment and loss of control. Norman (1980) identified the adaptive processes required to cope with residential care as precisely those that are less likely to be present in the people requiring residential care. Although the more recent increase in the numbers of residential care settings could arguably mean a greater choice, in practice the limitations, imposed by the under-resourcing of community care, ageist attitudes of professionals and the paternalistic way in which older people are often treated, suggest that this is a long way off for all but a minority who have the funds to choose.

The older person therefore enters residential care in a vulnerable state, as a consequence not only of the disability and losses they experience, but also of the fears they may have about what lies ahead. It is clear from this that the power to control and determine the individual older person's experience of that care lies with the institution and the staff who work in that institution. As a consequence of this, much research has focused on the experience of care for older people who live in such settings. This research has frequently found that, although there are areas of good practice where, as far as possible, the older person is empowered to make their environment as much like their home as is possible (Johnson, 1993; Peace *et al*, 1997), there are also clear examples of institutions where the routines and procedures are dictated by the institution and the staff within it. In this situation, when older people do not conform, they may be punished and abused, although it is clear that the staff may not view this as abuse, but rather as a way of getting through the work that needs to be done (Lee Treweek, 1994; Stannard, 1973; Meddaugh, 1993).

Risk Factors for Abuse in Institutions

Given the above information, one could be forgiven for viewing the older person as the helpless victim, and staff as monsters, as pointed out by Foner (1994). This author argues that to polarise the debate to this extent does not lead to our understanding why abuse occurs, and how this might be responded to. As in abuse within family settings, the factors leading to abuse are complex and multifaceted and require further exploration.

Pillemer (1988) proposed a theoretical model for maltreatment within nursing homes, which was first published in the UK by Glendenning (1997, pp159–160) (see Figure 12.1). He suggests that

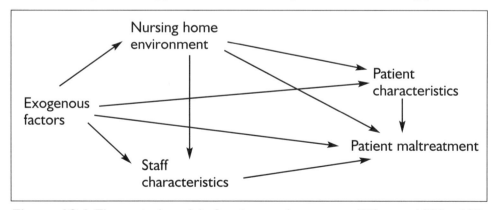

Figure 12.1 *Theoretical model of patient maltreatment (Pillemer, 1988: p230, cited by Glendenning [1997] with the author's permission)*

there are four major factors giving rise to the potential for abuse – nursing home environment, patient characteristics, staff characteristics and exogenous factors – and that these act together to create circumstances where abuse occurs. He offers this model as a guide to research, requiring exploration of the four variables. In this chapter, this framework will be used as a guide to understanding the factors that contribute to increased risk of elder abuse.

Exercise 12.1
Aim: to facilitate the reader's thinking on the factors that contribute to abuse within residential care settings.

The following case example provides a situation in a residential home where it is believed that abuse is occurring. Consider the factors in the case example, and list them under the following headings: (a) exogenous factors, (b) institutional environment, (c) resident characteristics and (d) staff characteristics. Following this, consider situations from your own experience and, if possible, add to the lists you have made.

Case Study

Mrs Callan has lived in a residential home for one year. She has always been an independent lady, who did not like to admit her need for help and, in fact, had managed extremely well, despite increasing problems, until six months before her admission, when her husband died. She arrived in care as a consequence of increasing disability following a number of cerebrovascular accidents (CVAs). These have left her with right-side weakness, including an inability to lift objects with her right hand or to dress herself, and she is unable to walk unaided. In addition, she has significant short-term memory loss, experiences periods of low mood and also suffers from incontinence, which she finds acutely embarrassing. Furthermore, her daughter is unable to provide the care she needs owing to her own living and work arrangements.

Despite these difficulties, Mrs Callan remains a psychologically independent woman who does not like her staff to take over and do everything for her. She receives only occasional visits from her daughter, who lives some 200 miles away. The home is often poorly staffed, with only one qualified member of staff on each shift, the others being auxiliaries. They appear to have little understanding of how to help the residents, and on one occasion the lady who shares a room with Mrs Callan sustained bruising as a result of inappropriate lifting. Mrs Callan was shouted at one night because she asked for the toilet outside the usual times. She complained to the nurse in charge the next day, but this was not acted upon as Mrs Callan was believed to be forgetful and over-sensitive.

From then on the night staff were hostile towards Mrs Callan. The trained nurse was rarely to be seen at night, mostly caring for the very ill older people. The care staff therefore shouldered most of the work, with little understanding of the residents' needs. They saw Mrs Callan as a troublemaker and would ignore her requests for help with toileting and getting ready for bed, often leaving her until last. If they perceived her as having been particularly demanding she would be given night sedation to 'calm her down'. Mrs Callan gradually became depressed and lethargic, rarely being allowed out of her room and becoming more dependent. She also became less communicative and was believed to have had another CVA.

Exogenous Factors

Pillemer (1988) suggests that some exogenous factors are likely to have an influence on the presence of abuse, although he further suggests that this has not been well researched and that he has therefore had to explore other literature. In the UK, a number of factors identified from related research also seem likely to affect the quality of care in some institutional settings. It has been pointed out by Fennell *et al* (1988) that the workers in the majority of institutional care settings are mainly female and low-paid. This is likely to reflect three trends. Firstly, the circumstances in which female labour is often organised may well mean that, owing to family commitments, women are prepared to accept lower standards of employment to bring home needed money (Finch & Groves, 1980). Secondly, this is further reinforced by the low status given to working with older people, which means that the workers themselves are often undervalued (Pietrukowicz et al, 1991). Finally, Peace et al (1997) also demonstrate that younger female workers often work in residential care because of failed career aspirations.

These three factors combine to mean that the employees are a 'captive workforce' in that they have limited alternative options for employment, a situation which may be further reinforced by high unemployment rates, and so they may be prepared to accept poor standards of employment and therefore caregiving. It also means that their need for training and support may not be adequately recognised and so fundamental issues of importance such as attitudes and approaches are not addressed.

Another subject raised by Pillemer (1988) in US research, is that of the supply of nursing homes in any given area which, if small, limits the choices open to older people and their families, so that they may have to accept places in homes which provide questionable care. This is equally applicable to the UK where, although the NHS and Community Care Act (1990) was designed to increase the options available to older people, in practice the uneven distribution in the development of residential and nursing home placements has meant that some areas have an excess, and so some older people may be able to exercise choice, while in other areas this is not possible (Bond, 1993).

Another factor which has an impact is that of the limited inspection and monitoring services available at present. As will be highlighted later, these are considered inadequate, even with the changes made recently, and they effectively mean that the opportunities to discover abuse, and to enforce penalties on an offending institution, are very limited. Institutions are 'closed' communities, frequently closed to the surrounding community, and with this and the reality of only two inspections a year, it becomes very easy to hide abusive behaviour (Meddaugh, 1993; Brammer, 1994; Peace et al, 1997).

Institutional Environment

As Pillemer (1988) points out, the environment is more than the physical surroundings of the home: it incorporates the organisational structure, the design of the home, the services provided and the financial resources. Willcocks *et al* (1987) have shown that the majority of homes that have been built more recently are large and, although the Department of Health has suggested that they should be built with homeliness in mind, in reality that has rarely been achieved. These authors further suggest that the large size of these homes tends to reinforce popular stereotypes of older people as disabled and incapable and does not encourage integration with the local community. The result is the isolation referred to previously.

Environments can also create circumstances in which mistreatment occurs by neglecting the design requirements of the individuals who live in them. Much work has been carried out which highlights how adaptations can be utilised to enhance independence and empower older people to remain self-reliant in the face of considerable disability. Johnson (1993) reports on the way in which group living incorporated into a homes design can achieve this. In addition, simple modifications such as clear signs, names on doors and directional arrows can make the difference between incontinence or independence in an older person with memory impairment (Stokes & Goudie, 1990).

However, the design of the environment can create problems not only for the older person, but also for staff. The lack of adequate facilities for responding to highly dependent older people can contribute to making the work harder and more stressful, which can lead to a more task-focused approach to care.

Environment also incorporates the organisational structure. Goffman's *Asylums* (1961) is undoubtedly one of the foremost publications on the impact of the institutional routine on the individuals who reside in them. The institution that ignores the needs of each individual, that imposes routines that are beneficial to the organisation rather than its residents, and that seeks to create circumstances in which individuality is denied through those routines increases the risk of abuse (Lee Treweek, 1994; Stannard, 1973; Meddaugh, 1993). It does this in ways that were referred to in Chapter 1, with older people being viewed as less than human and work as tasks to be got through. In this atmosphere, the older person who disrupts the routine can be seen to deserve punishment for 'misbehaving' (Lee Treweek, 1994).

It therefore follows that the attitudes of the managers of the residential establishment can have a considerable influence in determining the extent to which a non-custodial environment is promoted (Johnson, 1993; Willcocks *et al*, 1987). This will be reflected in their employment strategies, in terms of their staff-to-resident ratios and in the skill mix employed (Peace *et al*, 1997). Pillemer (1988) argues that homes which employ high levels of unqualified staff and have inadequate staff-to-resident ratios are more likely to abuse. The potential influence of managers is also reflected in their willingness to offer staff training and continuing development, including supervision (UKCC, 1994; Peace *et al*, 1997).

Staff Characteristics

It was indicated in Chapter 1 that staff who work with older people often hold ageist beliefs themselves. However, as Fennell *et al* (1988) suggest, we must go beyond this, and recognise that staff may be as much victims as the older people of the power of the institution, where they are often poorly paid and undervalued. Our culture does not place value on care work. Davies (1998) suggests that the construction of care in our culture is such that it is associated with emotional expression, which is viewed as a feminine trait and therefore one that is not valued. The consequences of this for care staff who are predominantly female is that their commitment to individuals is not valued and is seen as unnecessary. Dehumanising the older person may be the only way that they can come to terms with the impact of an institution which does not value their work.

Nevertheless, it is still important to recognise the nature of the relationship that occurs between staff and residents (Pillemer, 1988). As was highlighted earlier, the relationship between staff and residents is an unequal one, for many reasons. Older people come into residential care in a vulnerable state and therefore require positive responses from staff. It is argued that this is not always offered and that, in addition to the reasons given above, there are a number of reasons for this (Pillemer, 1988; Kitwood, 1997). Firstly, staff are confronted by fears about their own ageing and mortality on a daily basis. In a positive organisation, training may be offered to enable them to respond to these fears, but in a custodial organisation, in order to defend themselves against this daily confrontation, task-focused care may be resorted to. This may involve ignoring residents' emotional needs to get through the work that needs to be done and also the misuse of power to encourage passivity in residents (Lee Treweek, 1994; Meddaugh, 1993; Peace *et al*, 1997; Kitwood, 1997).

This is further reinforced by work carried out by Kitwood (1997) who identifies significant acts perpetrated by staff in the psychosocial environment which leads to depersonalisation and dehumanisation of the older person with dementia. He termed this 'Malignant Social Psychology' and argued that much of the negative care older people with dementia are subjected to arises out of a lack of knowledge and understanding of the experience of dementia for the older person. Also, and significantly, there is a lack of skills in communicating and making efforts to understand people's attempts at self-expression.

Secondly, it has been argued in many studies that much of the abuse in residential care is perpetrated by unqualified staff (Lee Treweek, 1994; Meddaugh, 1993, Foner, 1994; Stannard, 1973). Pillemer (1988) suggests that staff who have had little training are more likely to engage in abusive behaviour.

Thirdly, Pillemer and Moore (1989) found that abuse was more likely where staff experienced high levels of burnout. It can be argued that staff working in poor-quality residential settings experience many of the factors that lead to burnout. These include poor interpersonal support, high workload, exposure to patients with poor prognosis where the care staff do not receive appropriate support in managing their needs, high emotional demands and much of the time spent in direct contact with those patients (Schaufeli & Janczur, 1994).

Fourthly, Pillemer and Moore (1989) found in their study that staff were more likely to engage in abuse when there was a high level of conflict with residents. It would be very difficult to determine which came first in this sort of scenario: was the resident aggressive first, which led to hostile responses from staff, or was it the other way around? Indeed, to look for someone to blame is futile. It needs to be recognised that the behaviour is circular and relates to poor communication. However, it is clear from their study, and others, that staff who were not trained in managing difficult behaviour or in interpersonal skills, and who viewed the residents as childlike had difficulty in managing conflict and were more likely to resort to abuse (Stannard, 1973).

Resident Characteristics

A number of resident characteristics are thought to be associated with abuse. Many of the residents who enter care have significant disabilities, which may well include communication difficulties. It has been found by various authors, including Jones (1992), that nursing staff communicate less with residents who are impaired and interactions with them become more task-focused. Communication is a two-way process, with expectations held by both parties on the response that is required (Kitwood, 1997). Where difficulties are present, this exchange becomes unequal, and staff may not necessarily have the skills to adapt their style of communication to meet the needs of the resident.

Unfortunately, this lack of communication itself creates circumstances where depersonalisation of the resident is more likely. Indeed, Jones (1992) found that staff disliked residents with whom they could not communicate; their favourites tended to be those who were more alert and able to communicate and to thank the staff for their care. This depersonalisation means that staff are less likely to spend time with an individual and may experience conflict when carrying out personal care, as they have little understanding of how to meet the resident's needs.

As referred to earlier in this chapter, institutions are often isolated from the community, even when in a residential area. This is particularly true of the larger establishments, which may well be viewed with some alarm by the local community (Willcocks *et al*, 1987). This isolation, coupled with the losses that older people experience on admission, may well mean that the opportunities to receive visitors who could act as advocates on behalf of the older person are limited. In addition, the power relationship often means that older people and their relatives are reluctant to complain about the quality of their care. Stannard (1973) argues that, even if they do, they may not necessarily be taken seriously. Isolation is further enhanced by the fact that the opportunities for abuse often occur in private areas, where personal care is carried out, such as the bathroom or bedroom, where little help could be sought or evidence found (Lee Treweek, 1994; Meddaugh, 1993).

Key Points

In summary, it is clear that there are many risk factors associated with the abuse of older people in residential care. Pillemer & Moore (1989) suggest that previous research shows that the risk factors for abuse are the following: young staff, less well-educated staff, staff who are white, fewer years of experience of working within residential homes, and nursing assistants. They argue that these factors did not correlate with their research, and were more likely to be related to poor quality of care. The factors associated with deliberate abuse from their research were as follows:

1 poor job satisfaction,
2 viewing patients as childlike,
3 high levels of burnout,
4 high levels of conflict with the residents,
5 personal lives that are stressful,
6 high chance of verbal and physical assault by the resident,
7 poor wages,
8 physically taxing work,
9 low-prestige work,
10 no training in interpersonal skills.

However, as the authors point out, their research interviewed staff; the same interviews conducted with residents might result in a very different picture. Much of the qualitative research has shown that abuse within residential settings is often bound up with the routines of providing care (Lee Treweek, 1994; Meddaugh, 1993; Stannard, 1973; Foner, 1994). It is therefore often perceived not as abuse, but as a way of coping with the workload. For that very reason, intentional or not, poor-quality institutions are at greater risk of providing care which is abusive. Therefore many of the characteristics cited by Pillemer & Moore and previous research need to be considered when developing new residential or nursing home settings, when inspecting existing homes and, finally but most importantly, investigating suspected abuse.

Suggested Further Reading

Counsel and Care, 1992, *What if They Hurt Themselves*, Counsel and Care, London.

Department of Health, 1989, *Homes are for Living in,* HMSO, London.

Glendenning F, 1997, 'The mistreatment and neglect of elderly people in residential centres: research outcomes', in Decalmer P & Glendenning F (eds), *The Mistreatment of Elderly People,* 2nd edn, Sage, London.

Kitwood T, 1997, *Dementia Reconsidered*, Open University Press, Buckingham.

Lee Treweek G, 1994, 'Bedroom Abuse, the hidden work in a nursing home', *Generations Review Journal of the British Society of Gerontology* 4(1), pp2–4.

Peace S, Kellaher L & Willcocks D, 1997, *Re-evaluating Residential Care,* Open University Press, Buckingham.

Pillemer K, 1988, 'Maltreatment of Patients in Nursing Homes: Findings from a survey of staff', *The Gerontologist* 29(3), pp227–238.

Robb B, 1967, *Sans Everything; A case to answer?* Thomas Nelson, Edinburgh.

United Kingdom Central Council, 1994, *Professional Conduct: Occasional Report on Standards of Nursing in Nursing Homes* UKCC, London.

Willcocks D, Peace S & Kellaher L, 1987, *Private Lives in Public Places,* Tavistock, London.

CHAPTER 13

Prevention and Intervention

Introduction

The previous chapter demonstrated that the abuse of older people in institutional settings requires as comprehensive a response as that which occurs in domestic situations. It is therefore somewhat worrying to note that, despite inquiries such as that conducted by Southwark Social Services into Nye Bevan Lodge, little attention appears to have been paid to the recommendations of such reports and the implications of the information contained within them.

The intervention and prevention of abuse in these settings, as with other areas, lies at many different levels, and to focus purely on one aspect of this would be to deny the multifaceted responses that need to take place. However, as this book is concerned with intervention at a practice level, the present chapter will concern itself primarily with preventive measures designed to have a direct impact upon the presence of abuse, whether it be a potential threat or actually happening. The use of the local policies and procedures to intervene in situations where abuse is alleged should be the first line. However, it is believed that it is within the power of professionals working in and with homes, to influence and prevent much of the institutional abuse that occurs. This chapter reviews the Residential Homes Act 1984 in relation to the inspection and registration of homes in the United Kingdom, the new procedures suggested in the publication *Modernising Social Services* and the legal powers that local authorities and health authorities have in relation to the suspicion of abuse. The major focus of this chapter is then to explore the ways in which the factors referred to in the previous chapter can be responded to, in order to prevent the occurrence or recurrence of abuse.

The Residential Homes Act 1984

According to Brammer (1994), the number of residential homes in the UK increased from 1,871 in 1975 to 9,235 in 1992. Nursing homes also increased in number, from 1,000 in 1975 to 4,000 in 1992. This significant increase, coupled with the concomitant decrease in both NHS and local authority long-term care provision, has created a situation where the private and voluntary sectors are the largest providers of long-term care for older people in the UK (Peace *et al*, 1997). In practice, this means that, as people age, a greater number of them are likely to live in residential care. In the 85+ age range, 26 per cent of the older population live in care settings (Laing, 1995). It is therefore appropriate to explore the provisions that exist to monitor these institutions. The Residential Homes Act was first enacted in 1984 and reviewed in 1991. Under this Act, nursing and residential homes are required to register to provide care, even where the aim is only to provide two or three beds.

Registration requirements fall into three main areas, irrespective of the type of home: (a) both owner and manager have to be deemed 'fit' to run the home, (b) the premises have to be considered 'fit' for their purpose, (c) the facilities have to be adequate. (Small homes of only three or four beds only have to comply with the first requirement.) Failure to meet any of these requirements would result in a refusal of registration. Non-payment of the registration fee can also result in deregistration. The 1984 Act also required the homes to submit to regular inspection, with frequency being set at a minimum of twice per year; one of these should be announced and one unannounced. The inspections are intended to ensure that minimum standards are met, and the inspection officers have powers of entry. The 1990 NHS and Community Care Act further extended these powers to include 'arm's-length' inspection of local authority and NHS units, and a role in quality assurance. However, reviews of the effectiveness of the inspection offices have shown many inconsistencies (RCN, 1994). They further argue that the legislation is not robust enough and does not address issues of quality of care. The RCN (1994) report explored the inspection of nursing homes, and highlighted a number of concerns about the inspection units in health authorities.

- The inspectors are pressured to relinquish vigilance over homes that are good.
- The fees generated by registration do not cover the inspection fees.
- There is no upper limit to the number of visits and no stipulation on how these visits should be carried out.
- Some health authorities do not do the full range of checks on the fitness of an owner or manager.
- Where inspectors are involved in contracting, there is evidence of divided loyalties.
- There is no set guidance on the numbers of inspectors that should be employed.
- There is no set training for inspectors.

It is possible that these concerns may also be valid in local authority inspection units, and they point firmly to the need for greater co-ordination and consistency, with governmental guidance. The NHS and Community Care Act and the subsequent purchaser–provider split have engendered an increasing trend on the part of local authorities towards setting quality contracting standards. This has created the opportunity to influence care provision directly in contracted homes. However, the inadequacies of the current inspection system referred to earlier mean that the standards are difficult to monitor. This has resulted in the review of current regulatory systems in the government white paper, *Modernising Social Services* (1998), and the proposal of new arrangements. It was widely acknowledged that the present system does not protect people in the best way possible, and lacks a national response. The proposals are the following:

- to create Commissions for Care Standards, independent regional authorities responsible solely for the regulation of care services;
- to introduce new statutory regulation for services not currently covered, including domiciliary services;

- to improve the way in which registration and inspection are carried out. (Department of Health, 1998, 4.8.)

The Commissions will be independent and will create common standards for residential and nursing home care. They will monitor residential and nursing home care for adults as well as domiciliary care services. They will also be expected to provide training for inspectors and in developing more uniform processes for inspection, ensuring consistency across regions and the whole country. These proposals have yet to be made law and the current arrangements continue to exist until they do.

Preventing and Responding to Abuse

In the previous chapter, we explored the factors that might contribute to the risk of abuse in residential settings, utilising the model developed by Pillemer (1988). In exploring the presence of abuse in residential care, Johnson's (1991) definition, outlined in Chapter 2, is equally appropriate, and points to the need to explore interventions on a passive to aggressive continuum. Meddaugh (1993) further reinforces this by suggesting that, in some instances, identifying the guilty party may be less important than identifying the interventions that can break the cycle. With this in mind this section will return to three of the four factors identified by Pillemer, to explore both intervention and prevention.

The Institutional Environment

The issues of structure, staffing, design, attitudes and routines were addressed as factors contributing to the risk of abuse in the previous chapter. These aspects are particularly significant in preventing and intervening in elder abuse. Probably the most important issue to address initially is that of the attitudes of the organisation. Brammer (1994) has raised concerns about the orientation of managers of the homes in seeing them purely as a business. Clearly, the owner/manager needs to have business skills, the absence of which would endanger the residents' quality of life, however, the primary motivation needs to be that of providing high-quality care to the older people who reside there, rather than doing it purely as a business. This should be reflected in the policies, procedures and practices of the organisation. It is argued that this can be achieved through many different methods. For example, the report *Homes are for Living In* (1989) provided standards for care settings that seek to measure these particular issues. The standards identify the means by which homes can achieve supportive practices including offering privacy, dignity, independence and choice. Key to this is the prevailing attitudes of the managers of the care setting.

Exercise 13.1
Aim: to enable the reader to identify the values through which an organisation can promote an environment that reduces the risk of abuse.

The following statements are quotations from research that has worked in identifying the factors that relate to high standards of care, although these statements reflect evidence of both good and bad care. Having read them, note down the principles that you believe should be prevalent in the attitudes of the organisation.

Pointing the resident to the handrail is much more important than propping her up personally. If the staff make this early mistake, Miss Webb will always be looking to the staff for assistance. It is all too easy to create dependence within the first few hours. (Johnson, 1993, p125)

Perhaps fundamental to this regime was the belief of the officer in charge that residents wanted and were able to continue to involve themselves in ordinary and familiar activities. From the start she had selected staff who could share and implement her convictions. (Ibid, p126)

You lose your independence when you come to these places ... I'll never be happy here, but I'll have to stick it because I won't live long, much longer. (Hockey, 1989, p206)

> Under present institutional arrangements, there is an implicit organisational commitment to a form of task allocation which promotes staff surveillance and the avoidance of risk taking. (Willcocks et al, 1987, p155)

> Whilst 90% of the homes had handrails along the corridors, nearly one in five homes had corridors that were interrupted by steps ... a definite hindrance to mobility. (Wilcocks et al, 1987, p97)

> Where I was I didn't feel that I was a human being ... all my responsibilities were taken away from me. I even went to the loo when they told me to ... Where I am living now I control my own life and no one tells me what to do. One of the main things that makes the difference is the philosophy of facilitation, which means the staff are our arms and legs. It means I can control my own life. (NISW, 1988a, p148)

Perhaps the single most important factor is the culture in which the care is given. This involves and includes managers who are committed to organisational development and quality assurance systems which monitor and improve on the delivery of care. Many authors suggest that quality assurance can do much to create a culture in which the residents and staff feel not only that they are listened to and that their views and concerns are acted upon, but also that they are empowered to influence the care that is given (Peace et al, 1997; Wright, 1992). This culture requires a positive attitude towards working with older people, and a fundamental belief in their right to high standards of care.

It is suggested that this positive approach can be found in settings that have adopted a number of important practices. First is a charter of rights for residents (UKCC, 1994). Many organisations have charters, but do not necessarily monitor their effectiveness in achieving rights for residents. These charters need to be linked with quality assurance programmes. Second is clear policies and procedures that reflect the values of the organisation and which respond to individual need, not blanket approaches (Counsel and Care, 1992; Seaton, 1994).

Successive reports have highlighted the lack of individual focused care. They also comment on the application of practices which seek to maintain and indeed create dependence in the residents. This is clearly not acceptable. Homes are for living in, but should seek to support the individual in maintaining independence; that is, having a focus which is enabling rather than dependence-creating. The possibility that an individual could return to living in a community setting should not necessarily be discounted as soon as they cross the threshold of residential care. This should also include the capacity to meet the varied needs of an individual. Proposals in *Modernising Social Services* include the potential to make dual registration easier, which is a welcome step forward in meeting complex needs.

A third requirement is a rolling programme of quality assurance, such as inside quality assurance or dementia care mapping, which measures the process as well as the outcomes of care, and involves older people and their families in the evaluation of the care (Wright, 1992; Kitwood, 1997; Raynes,1999; Hollingbery, 1999). This should include the reality that quality of life of residents may well be different from quality of care. Measures should seek to determine what would be required to improve quality of life for residents, rather than just focusing on standards relating to the care offered. Kitwood (1997) highlights this with care of people with dementia, where care, however well meaning, can cause harm if consideration is not given to the individual and how they would like to be treated.

A fourth requirement is accurate and up-to-date record keeping, in which staff can justify their actions (UKCC, 1994; Meddaugh, 1993). Individualised care plans, which include information on the clients' history, and likes and dislikes, create opportunities to enhance client care. This is particularly the case where the clients have difficulty in communicating their needs owing to conditions such as dementia.

A fifth requirement is a training programme, which involves training staff in, amongst other things, interpersonal skills, conflict resolution, interpersonal stress and how to manage the needs of the residents (Pillemer & Hudson, 1993). The provision of training and development through National Vocational Qualifications (NVQs) has increased over the past decade. Many contracting procedures stipulate the requirement for staff to carry this out, but, without the organisational commitment to empower staff to use the skills developed, and systems and support that actively require this, these can become paper qualifications with little meaning in practice.

Sixth, there should be an active recruitment and retention programme, which seeks to value staff, through consultation, empowerment, and meet the needs of older people through numbers of staff employed and the skill mix.

Seventh, residents' relatives and friends should be involved, if possible even prior to admission, in the care of the older person. Many relatives, particularly carers, struggle with the decision to place someone in residential care. This may manifest itself in complaints against the staff. Every effort should be made to involve and include the relatives and friends in the process of admission and subsequent care offered. They are a valuable source of information about the person, and maintain continuity with their history and sense of self.

Eighth, there should be a clear complaints and comments procedure, which is made known to every resident. Ninth, staff managerial and clinical supervision should be provided. Tenth, there should be admission procedures which empower the older person to make choices as far as is possible. Finally, links should be maintained with the residents' community and networks following admission.

Essentially, it is argued that organisations need to be client-centred in their practice. To be anything else encourages a task-focused approach to care, which risks dehumanising and destroying self-esteem in residents who are already vulnerable. Overall, the organisation needs to show commitment to its customers, in terms of its willingness to be flexible about the changing needs of residents and therefore the need to alter the structure, process and outcomes of care as appropriate.

Staff Characteristics
It was suggested in the previous chapter that staff are as likely to be victims of the organisation as the residents are. Areas where this might be the case, such as the lack of training offered to unqualified staff and

the lack of opportunity to influence practice for the better in large institutions, which may lead to stress, were identified in Chapter 12. It has been argued that many of the conditions that staff have to work under in residential care create circumstances in which high levels of burnout are experienced (Carson *et al*, 1995; Pillemer, 1989; Schaufeli & Janczur, 1994).

Many authors indicate that unqualified staff are particularly at risk of abusing the residents, as they are likely to have most contact with them (Lee Treweek, 1994; Stannard, 1973; Pillemer & Moore, 1989). Much of the reason for this, it is suggested, is their lack of understanding of the care required by the residents, and their inability to manage situations in which the resident has needs which are beyond their coping skills and where conflict arises. This can all be responded to by using the suggestions made in the previous section.

First and foremost, staff need to feel that they are valued, and that their views are taken into account. This can be achieved via a number of strategies. Wright (1992) suggests that quality assurance should be a 'bottom up' approach. It has been demonstrated that involving staff in quality assurance programmes can empower and involve them in making changes and gaining satisfaction from their work. The development of staff should be a fundamental principle. Working with older people is not just common sense and requires skills which many people entering the caring field for the first time do not have.

Pillemer & Hudson (1993) found that an established training programme which explores issues such as interpersonal skills, dealing with challenging behaviour, the direct confrontation of the nature of abuse, why it occurs and prevention strategies, all had an influence on the presence of abusive behaviour in those staff. This would seem to be particularly necessary where staff are working with highly dependent older people who may have dementia and/or experience significant communication problems. The opportunities for depersonalising people such as this, particularly when their behaviour is challenging and requires time that is not available, are great. In these circumstances the staff need to be taught how to communicate with the individual older person, in ways such as those described by Kitwood (1997), Pietrukowicz *et al* (1991) and Jones (1992).

To prevent burnout, it is suggested by authors such as Farrington (1995) that the use of group work and stress counselling, in which the participants are encouraged openly to discuss the emotional aspects of their work with residents, can effect a reduction in stress and sickness levels. The UKCC (1994) also argue for the implementation of supervision in homes where nurses practise. It is suggested here that clinical supervision be offered to all staff, irrespective of grade, as a means by which staff can be supported, nurtured, developed and valued. In addition, supervision provides opportunities for staff to develop their knowledge of ways of managing individual residents, which can decrease the risk of responding in an abusive manner.

Despite the focus on unqualified staff, it must be stated that the qualified staff, whether they be nurses, social workers or others, also require similar forms of support. The UKCC (1994) clearly identified the need for a more vigilant approach in residential and nursing home care as a consequence of the numbers of staff being seen by the Professional Conduct Committee. This need is also identified in *Modernising Social Services* (1998), where proposals include the development of mechanisms to set and enforce standards of practice amongst care staff. Working in institutions can be and often is an isolating experience, with limited opportunities for updating and development. These staff also require the support and commitment of management to enable them to provide high-quality care.

Patient Characteristics
In exploring the ways in which care can be developed to provide an environment that is free from abuse, the characteristics of patients or residents also need to be considered. Chapter 4 explored the meaning and significance of relationships in later life, highlighting how important relationships are to us in terms of our self-esteem. As has already been indicated, much of the research highlights how many residents lose contact with significant friends and community on admission to care. It is not surprising, therefore, that residents place a significant emphasis on the interpersonal environment and the extent to which it meets their emotional needs.

Milburn *et al* (1995) have researched the characteristics that are most valued by patients in hospital. Many of these, such as staff having time to listen, conveying concern and understanding, the need to have a social environment in which the patient feels comfortable and safe, emphasise the importance of staff taking psychological needs of patients into account. Lee Treweek (1994) found that patients with emotional needs were often ignored, or viewed as moaners. Perhaps, if staff were given the opportunity and the skills to meet some of their emotional needs, they would not be viewed as inappropriately demanding of staff time. The use of creative means of engaging residents in activity and stimulation, both within their local community and in the home itself, is identified by Peace *et al* (1997) as being significant in the experience of positive care. The use of strategies such as resolution therapy, referred to in Chapter 10, and individual and group-focused activity could do much to enhance the relationship between staff and residents, thus lessening the objectifying of people which is so common in abusive environments.

Goffman (1961) highlighted the impact of institutionalisation on the individual, and the resulting behaviour disturbances that some individuals developed. If staff were encouraged to enable older people to maintain their independence and their social identities, through the use of such work as life histories, it is possible that the risk of abuse would be lessened.

Key Points

Much of this chapter has focused on the means by which abuse can be prevented in residential and nursing care settings. This approach has considerable value in highlighting that much can be done at an individual and organisational level. Intervention, particularly in serious cases, needs to be assessed on an individual basis, and the application of procedures such as adult protection guidelines are equally important and valuable for abuse which occurs in these settings. The use of intervention strategies such as those outlined in Chapter 10 is also important in responding to the individual who has been abused.

Abuse within residential care settings is as much a matter for concern as abuse within the family. Organisations have within their grasp, as do individual members of staff, the power to influence good practice. However, it also needs to be acknowledged that this issue should be responded to at a much wider level than it has been hitherto, with standards produced and monitored to facilitate effective care which allows residents to live in circumstances which are free from abuse.

Suggested Further Reading

Centre for Environment and Social Studies in Ageing, 1992, *Inside Quality Assurance*, Information Design Unit, Newport Pagnell.

Department of Health, 1998, *Modernising Social Services* Cmnd 4169, The Stationery Office, London.

Jones G & Miesen BML, 1992, *Caregiving in Dementia, Research and Applications,* Routledge, London.

Kitwood T, 1997, *Dementia Reconsidered, the Person Comes First,* Open University Press, Buckingham.

Kohner N, 1994, *Clinical Supervision in Practice,* Kings Fund Centre, London.

NISW 1988, *Residential Care: A Positive Choice*, Wagner Report, HSMO, London.

Peace S, Kellaher L & Willcocks D, 1997, *Re-evaluating Residential Care,* Open University Press, Buckingham.

Pillemer K & Hudson B, 1993, 'A Model Abuse Prevention Programme for Nursing Assistants', *The Gerontologist* 33(1), pp128–131.

Part 5

Contextual Issues

CHAPTER 14

Professional Issues

Introduction

Abuse is both a multifaceted and multidimensional issue encompassed within legal, sociocultural, political, moral, religious, psychological and medical domains. Although for many cultures, the abuse of vulnerable people is deplored, it remains a taboo subject often being swept under the carpet. It is also an area of human functioning that is neither well defined nor well understood and can take various forms within different contexts. As a consequence, working with abuse can pose considerable challenges to professionals and associated agencies alike.

Identifying Abuse

The identification of abuse can in itself pose particular difficulties even for experienced practitioners, for various reasons. Firstly, whilst there are clearly defined features or symptoms which are associated with abuse (Johnson, 1991), the presentation of such features is not always evident in all cases. In addition, presenting features may in themselves be symptomatic of other illnesses or experiences unrelated to abuse. For example, a fall may cause significant bruising to the face and give rise to psychological manifestations related to an acute stress reaction such as sleeplessness, withdrawal, agitation, fear, poor appetite and depressed mood all of which are also symptomatic of physical assault.

Secondly, in a small number of cases where the client discloses abuse, the reliability of such information may be problematic, particularly if that client is experiencing delusions or other psychotic symptoms, or in cases of memory loss where the client may attribute their feelings to having been abused by a relative or professional. The final factor pertains to the extent to which a professional's opinion and judgement may be influenced by their own values, attitude or stereotypes concerning abuse and mistreatment.

Whilst the typology of abusive acts is definable, the actual acknowledgement of such acts as being abusive is often influenced by issues relating to the intent of the perpetrator committing such an act, the social and psychological circumstances surrounding the act and the impact the act has upon the victim. The following example illustrates this issue.

Mrs Wilson had been suffering from a dementing illness for several years and had been attending day care so that respite could be afforded to her husband. The couple has been married for 55 years and Mr Wilson was taking the primary caregiving role. Over a period of several months, Mrs Wilson was observed by the day care staff increasingly to wander about the premises and to become progressively more reluctant to eat her meals. Concern was raised by the staff as to how Mr Wilson was able to manage, since the staff themselves were having considerable difficulty. When the issue was addressed with Mr Wilson, he reported that he was not experiencing difficulties as he would secure his wife to the dining chair, using various ropes and belts, which enabled him to feed her. He further reported that he was not aware of his wife becoming distressed by his actions, and that he would release her following completion of the meal.

The circumstances were brought to the case conference, whereupon discussion took place as to whether Mr Wilson's action constituted abuse and, if so, what would be the most appropriate response.

The discussion centred around the caregiver's intent in acting as he did, the impact it had upon his wife and the circumstances surrounding the act. One view was that, since Mr Wilson's intention was to ensure that his wife was properly fed, given that her condition precluded her from feeding herself independently, and that in any event it did not seem to distress her, the act did not constitute abuse.

Nevertheless, other ways of feeding Mrs Wilson should be explored with her husband.

An alternative view was that, while Mr Wilson's actions, on the surface, may appear to have been prompted by a desire to ensure his wife's well-being, they possibly reflected an underlying problem he had in coming to terms with the loss of their previous relationship. That is, the act was a symbolic manifestation of Mr Wilson's need to retain intimacy and control within the relationship. Consequently, counselling should be offered to Mr Wilson to help him come to terms with the transition and develop alternative ways of meeting this need, should this continue to be an issue following counselling.

A third viewpoint was proposed which held that, irrespective of the reasons for Mr Wilson restraining his wife in this way, or whether or not she showed obvious distress, an abusive act had been perpetrated and, as a consequence, an adult protection procedure should be instigated. Issues of intent, circumstances and the impact upon Mrs Wilson should be considered as part of the formal protection procedure and should not influence the team's decision as to whether or not the act constituted abuse.

The above example clearly illustrates the dilemma many professionals face in determining abuse. This dilemma often arises, not because of ignorance concerning the act itself since, as mentioned previously, typologies were readily available, but, rather because professionals hold discrepant opinions on what characteristics influencing various acts should be considered in determining whether or not they are abusive. That is, while an act may technically fall within the typology of abuse, such acts are not considered as abusive since intent, circumstances and the impact of abuse upon the individual mitigate against such an interpretation.

One argument would suggest that such discrepant views are valuable, in that they allow full consideration and addressing of individuals' circumstances and, in addition, promote the development of therapeutic alliances with the client at an early stage. An alternative argument would suggest that, unless a standardised approach among professionals in both acknowledging and responding to abuse is applied, further acts of abuse may go undetected.

A third view may be applied, extrapolating from both of the previous arguments, which would suggest that a standardised approach to abuse identification and acknowledgement is applied in the first instance. This is irrespective of circumstances, intent or impact since this guards against the possibility of professional values overriding the rights of an individual to proper protection and appropriate care. Decisions concerning further action would then incorporate the other issues, preferably following discussion with other relevant parties, where this is possible.

Client Identification
Defining the client is of primary importance in cases where the nature of the therapeutic relationship requires strict boundaries of confidentiality and advocacy. Arguably, it is professionally inappropriate, for example, for any single individual to provide a service to both victim and perpetrator where their needs may be either discordant or incompatible with each other. To do so might compromise professional boundaries and therapeutic allegiances. Consequently, consideration needs to be given to the most appropriate level or 'client system' in which to focus intervention. This may be the victim themselves, the perpetrator, the couple as a single subsystem, or the wider family system.

Decision making concerning the above is likely to be based on a number of central issues: the most appropriate focus for change in terms of influence and responsibility; the immediacy of factors maintaining abusive behaviour; the extent to which the client may be 'protected' in their natural or social environment. In addition, the theoretical orientation of the therapist is likely to play an important role in terms of their preferred working models and practices, professional experience and access to relevant supervision. Those who involve the family as a single client or seek to work with the individual client within their wider family context should do so with an understanding of systems theory.

Client Access
It is often assumed that clients are willing and able to seek help in resolving abuse. In reality, however, gaining access to clients for help

and treatment is rarely straightforward. Many individuals and families are reluctant to disclose or acknowledge abuse, even when the available evidence suggests that abuse is taking place (Lau & Kosberg, 1979). There may be several reasons for this. Firstly, disclosure of abuse may lead to further and more severe abuse by the perpetrator. Secondly, such disclosure may lead to the perpetrator withholding the very support which the victim depends upon for their care. Thirdly, it may lead to dislocation or break-up of the family unit. Fourthly, the perpetrator themselves may fear being negatively evaluated or judged by professionals, with possible legal ramifications. Fifthly, there may be inherent cultural rules and expectations concerning disclosure. Finally, a client may have an inherent distrust of formal services. As a result, the possibility of a client's agreement to service intervention is likely to be minimised. In addition, in cases where help is sought, the client may present their need for help in ways other than directly disclosing or acknowledging that abuse is taking place.

Factors Affecting Therapeutic Objectivity

Crucial to a successful course of treatment is the extent to which the therapist or support worker is able to offer their client a therapeutic relationship which is free from judgement or prejudice. Where the issue of therapy is one which holds few, if any, emotional associations for the therapist, objectivity is unlikely to become a problem. However, where that issue is related to the therapist's prior personal experiences or where the issue in itself holds powerful emotional connotations, objectivity may be difficult to attain. Indeed, if the emotional association goes unrecognised, a negative transference may ensue where the therapist's feelings, conflicts and needs become displaced upon the client.

Abuse is an emotive issue for most people, one which challenges the very basis of human dignity. In cases where the impact of abuse is particularly devastating for the client, or where the therapist may have been subject to abuse themselves, their ability to provide a non-judgemental, non-prejudicial service is likely to be severely challenged. It is therefore important that the therapist be aware of their idiosyncratic cognitions and emotions concerning abuse, that they are not bringing into the therapeutic relationship unresolved conflicts relating to their own experiences of abuse, and that they are therefore clear regarding the motives they have for working in this complex and highly emotive area.

Inter-Agency and Multidisciplinary Teamwork

The nature and complexity of issues which have to be addressed in abuse work necessitates a multidisciplinary and inter-agency approach. In addition to the availability and co-ordination of multimodal input for assessment, problem identification and resolution, teamwork also provides a mechanism for interpersonal support, supervision and training.

However, multidisciplinary and multi-agency teamwork is not without its problems. Firstly, as Wolf & Pillemer (1989) point out, co-operation is of central importance if the team is to function effectively and meet its goals. Co-operation, by its very nature, implies the need for open and congruent communication, acknowledgement of the strengths and limitations of each agency or professional involved and a willingness to adopt a democratic rather than autocratic style. This should be applied to operational procedures in decision-making processes irrespective of who may hold principal accountability in the overall care of the client. It is important, therefore, that these issues are addressed appropriately by the team prior to client engagement and, where possible, it is advisable that some form of retrospective auditing of the team's processes occur following client discharge in order to ascertain areas for further development.

Secondly, there needs to exist a well-defined and accepted set of operational procedures. These procedures denote clearly the membership of the team or involved agencies, the various roles and responsibilities they carry, the nature of relationships and levels of accountability inherent among members and what actions may be required should such procedures break down.

Thirdly, whilst any team can be seen as being greater than the sum of its parts, individuals necessarily bring with them their own idiosyncratic ways of operating within group settings. In part, this involves the influence of professional training in terms of views, practices, goals and responsibilities. Although this may be seen as a positive influence in decision making, there may exist intrapersonal variables related to an individual's particular attitude and feelings towards abuse, their ability to engage social situations and the extent to which they may be experiencing stress or related problems as a result of wider personal or social difficulties. Where such issues become incompatible with effective team functioning, it is important that they are raised with the individual concerned and that appropriate courses of action are taken to resolve the problems.

Finally, Riley (1989) focuses upon the need for trust between agencies and team members. She points out: 'We cannot deal effectively with elder abuse without mutual respect.' Of particular importance are the trust individuals hold regarding confidentiality of information, the designated courses of action to be carried out appropriately, individuals' willingness to continue to participate in multidisciplinary case conferences and respect for each profession or agency represented within the team.

Recommendations for Therapeutic Practice

Given the above issues, the following recommendations are offered in support of quality practices.

1 That professionals have a clear understanding concerning both legal and contractual obligations as they affect their work with their client. This is particularly relevant where issues of confidentiality and the reporting of abuse are concerned.
2 That clear lines of accountability, responsibility and working practices are delineated across professionals and involved agencies.
3 That professionals have a clear understanding concerning both adult protection procedures and the circumstances in which the commencement of such procedures should occur.
4 That professionals have substantive knowledge and understanding of abuse as it operates within the client's social and cultural context.
5 That professionals have both substantive knowledge and experience in identifying signs and symptoms of abuse and, in particular, being able to abstract relevant information attributable to possible abuse from that which may be attributable to other causes.
6 That, prior to engaging treatment in this area, the 'client' is clearly identified, along with the specific remit of work to be undertaken.

7   That, in cases where the therapeutic relationship may be adversely influenced by a client's mental state or behaviour, communication difficulties, negative transference or counter-transference, consideration should be given to having the assistance of a co-therapist or supervisor in order to ensure appropriate professional practices and to ensure that the rights and security of both the client and the therapist are properly addressed.

8   That the right of a client to refuse treatment for whatever reason and at any given point during treatment should always be respected. However, there may be circumstances where the client's decision to refuse is influenced by limited awareness, perceived threat as a consequence of intervention or prolonged distress experienced during intervention. In such cases it is advisable that the professional discusses such issues with the client or associated worker and where possible develop a strategy for addressing relevant difficulties. Where this cannot be done, the professional should disclose their concerns to the client or associated worker and offer advice regarding possible alternatives.

9   That where abuse continues to be apparent, either at the onset of or during treatment, consideration should be given to whether continuation of such treatment is advisable or recourse to protection procedures should be considered as a priority.

10 That professionals are clear in themselves regarding any prejudices, emotional associations or unresolved conflicts they may have regarding abuse which might interfere with their professional duties. It is therefore advisable that prior to engaging in abuse work, professionals undergo a period of formal self-exploration and that they are satisfied beyond doubt of their eligibility to practise in this field.

CHAPTER 15

Conclusion: Towards a Comprehensive Response

THIS BOOK HAS BEEN WRITTEN with the intention of enabling the practitioner to gain a greater knowledge of elder abuse, and the means through which older people, their families and their carers can be approached in situations where abuse is suspected.

It has not been the aim of this book to answer all the questions; indeed, it is likely that it will have raised many further questions, at individual, organisational or societal levels, which require answering. In particular, such issues as the abuse of ethnic minority have not been specifically addressed owing to the paucity of research available. However, it was intended to provide the practitioner with an increased awareness, and also the knowledge that action is possible: action within the scope of each practitioner, each organisation and society as a whole, to respond and give to older people the attention to which they have a right. Accordingly, this final chapter is devoted to summarising the key points made throughout the book, with statements that can be used as pointers to developing good practice.

Reframing the Social Construction of Elder Abuse
This book has highlighted the dangers inherent in attitudes that either ignore the existence of elder abuse, view it as an acceptable response to the stress engendered by the older person's dependency, or see it as appropriate to develop responses based on a child abuse framework. Accordingly, a number of principles should be borne in mind in relation to both organisational and individual attitudes towards this issue.

1   While abuse is an ordinary life experience, it is a legitimate service issue. This is particularly the case where the older person is unable to protect themselves, and where the continuation of the abuse affects physical, psychological and social well-being.

2   The experience of abuse needs to be viewed within a wider social and ageist culture, which acknowledges that many older people are subject to abuse at the hands of society as a whole, and that it is not an experience that is purely medically defined.

3   Older people have the right to live freely, without abuse, and with their needs for safety and security met.

4   The individual older person should determine what is abusive for themselves, as far as is possible.

5   Responses should acknowledge and be sensitive to racial, cultural and individual diversification.

6   The development of practice and procedures should be positive (that is, non-judgemental and non-discriminatory).

7   Abuse should be considered as a product of relational dynamics and life cycle transitions, not as being the result of an individual's characteristics.

The Development of a Service Culture

Further to the above principles which should inform attitudes, it is suggested that, to respond to abuse effectively, the culture of services, either currently being developed or already in existence, needs to incorporate a number of operational standards, including the following:

1   Awareness and assessment of elder abuse, irrespective of the principal needs or issues that a service may address.

2   Active promotion and maintenance of inter-agency multi-professional co-operation when working with elder abuse.

3   Clearly defined operational procedures and standards for responding to elder abuse.

4   Availability of a keyworker mechanism for providing a continuous relationship between clients and service provider.

5   Empowering of clients through involvement in decision making about service provision and through a formal complaints procedure.

6   A formalised training strategy for all grades of staff which incorporates personal development plans and supervision.

The Provision of Intervention Systems

Finally, in keeping with the aim of this book, which was to enable practitioners to explore their working practices with older people who experience abuse, it suggests that intervention systems should work towards the following:

1   Abuse prevention and maintenance of an abuse-free life, as well as intervention in cases of actual elder abuse.
2   Providing the means to empower people on the resident's behalf for the purposes of protection, but which are minimally invasive; that is, only in those areas where an individual is incapable of action themselves.
3   Empowering the client to make decisions concerning those interventions which the client construes as being appropriate and to be implemented at the client's own pace.
4   Having the capacity to meet different clients' needs within a single or multiple system.
5   Creativity in the use and range of interventions.
6   Having a proven track record in the achievement of successful outcomes.

Working with older people, their families and their carers where abuse is suspected is neither simple nor straightforward. It requires creativity and a willingness on the part of services to acknowledge that elder abuse exists and that it has equal status with other forms of violence such as child abuse in requiring a co-ordinated and comprehensive response. Older people have the right to be free from abuse in all its forms.

Bibliography

Albert SM, 1991, 'Cognition of Caregiving Tasks, Multidimensional Scaling of the Caregiver Task Domain', *The Gerontologist* 31(6), pp726–734.

Albert SM, 1992, 'Psychometric Investigation of a Belief System, Caregiving to the Chronically Ill Parent', *Social Sciences Medicine* 35(5), pp699–709.

Aneschensel CS, Pearlin LI & Schuler RH, 1993, 'Stress, Role Captivity and the Cessation of Caregiving', *Journal of Health and Social Behaviour* 34 (March), pp54–70.

Archbold PG, Stewart BJ, Greenlick MR & Harvath T, 1990, 'Mutuality and Preparedness as Predictors of Caregiver Role Strain', *Research in Nursing and Health* 13, pp375–384.

Baker AA, 1975, 'Granny Battering', *Modern Geriatrics* 8, pp20–24.

Baumgarten M *et al*, 1992, 'The Psychological and Physical Health of Family Members Caring for an Elderly Person With Dementia', *Journal of Clinical Epidemiology* 45(1), pp61–70.

Bendik MF, 1992, 'Reaching the Breaking Point: Dangers of Mistreatment in Elder Caregiving Situations', *Journal of Elder Abuse and Neglect* 4(3), pp39–59.

Bennett G, 1990a, 'Action on Elder Abuse in the 90's, A new definition will help', *Geriatric Medicine* April, pp53–55.

Bennett G, 1990b, 'Abuse of the Elderly: prevention and legislation', *Geriatric Medicine* October, pp55–60.

Bennett G & Kingston P, 1993, *Elder Abuse, Concepts, Theories and Interventions,* Chapman & Hall, London.

Berg-Cross L, 1997, *Couples Therapy,* Sage, London.

Biggs S, 1993, *Understanding Ageing, Images Attitudes and Professional Practice,* Open University Press Buckingham.

Bond J, 1993, 'Living Arrangements of Elderly People', Bond J & Coleman P (eds), *Ageing in Society: An Introduction to Social Gerontology,* Sage, London.

Boszormenyi-Nagy I & Ulrich DN, 1980, 'Contextual Family Therapy',Gurman AS & Kniskern DP (eds), *Handbook of Family Therapy,* Bruner Mazel, New York.

Bowlby J, 1980, *Attachment and Loss: Sadness and Depression,* vol 3, Penguin, London.

Brammer A, 1994, 'The Registered Homes Act 1984: Safeguarding The Elderly?', *Journal of Social Welfare and Family Law* 4, pp423–437.

Breckman RS & Adelman RD, 1988, *Strategies for Helping Victims of Elder Mistreatment,* Sage, Thousand Oaks.

Brody EM & Schoonover CB, 1989, 'Caregiving Daughters and their Local Siblings: Perceptions, Strains and Interactions', *The Gerontologist* 29(4), pp529–538.

Butler RN, 1963, 'The Life Review, An Interpretation of Reminiscence in the Aged', *Psychiatry* 26, pp65–76.

Bytheway B, 1995, *Ageism,* Open University Press, Buckingham.

Bytheway B & Johnson J, 1990, 'On defining Ageism', *Critical Social Policy* 27, pp27–39.

Callahan D, 1987, *Setting Limits, Medical Goals in an Ageing Society,* Simon & Schuster, New York.

Carson J, Fagin L & Ritter S, 1995, 'Stress in Mental Health Nurses: Comparison of Ward and Community Staff', *British Journal of Nursing* 4(10), pp579–582.

Carter B & McGoldrick M, 1989, *The Changing Family Life Cycle: a Framework for Family Therapy,* Allyn and Bacon, Boston.

Cobe GM, 1985, 'The Family of the Aged: Issues in Treatment', *Psychiatric Annals* 15, pp343–347.

Cohen CA, Gold DP, Schulman II, Wortley JT, McDonald DG & Wargon M, 1993, 'Factors Determining the Decision to Institutionalise Dementing Individuals: A Prospective Study', *The Gerontologist* 33(6), pp714–720.

Coleman P, 1993, 'Psychological Ageing', Bond J & Coleman P (eds), *Ageing in Society: an Introduction to Social Gerontology,* Sage, London.

Collingridge M, 1993, 'Contested Concepts, Protection of the Elderly: some Legal and Ethical Issues', *Australian Journal on Ageing* 12(4), pp32–35.

Conkey D & Woodford-Williams E, 1979, 'Effects of Burglary and Vandalism on the Health of Old People', *The Lancet* 8151, pp1066–1067.

Cook FL, Skogan FL, Cook TD & Antunes GE, 1978, 'Criminal Victimisation of the Elderly, The Physical and Economic Consequences', *The Gerontologist* 18(4), pp338–349.

Counsel and Care, 1992, *Not such Private Places,* Counsel and Care, London.

Craig Y, 1992, 'Elder Mediation', *Generations Review, Journal of the British Society of Gerontology* 2(3), pp4–5.

Craig Y, 1995, 'Empowerment not Empire Building', *Generations Review, Journal of the British Society of Gerontology* 5(1), pp7–9.

Dahl R, 1983, *Dirty Beasts,* Picture Puffin, London.

Davies C, 1998, 'Caregiving, Carework and Professional Care', Brechin A, Walmsley J, Katz J & Peace S (eds), *Care Matters, Concepts, Practice and Research in Health and Social Care,* Sage, London.

Davies M, 1993, 'Recognising Abuse: An Assessment Tool for Nurses', Decalmer P & Glendenning F (eds), *The Mistreatment of Elderly People,* Sage, London.

Decalmer P, 1993, 'Clinical Presentation', Decalmer P & Glendenning F (eds) *The Mistreatment of Elderly People,* Sage, London.

Decalmer P & Marriot A, 1993, 'The Multidisciplinary Assessment of Clients and Patients', Decalmer P & Glendenning F (eds), *The Mistreatment of Elderly People,* Sage Press, London.

Department of Health, 1998, *Modernising Social Services,* Cmnd 4169, The Stationery Office, London.

Dryden W & Rentoull R, 1991, *Adult Clinical Problems, A Cognitive Behavioural Approach,* Routledge, London.

Duck S, 1992, *Human Relationships,* 2nd edn, Sage, Thousand Oaks.

Eastman M, 1982, 'Granny Battering, a Hidden Problem', *Community Care* 413, p27.

Eastman M, 1984, *Old Age Abuse,* Age Concern, Portsmouth.

Epstein NB & Bishop DS, 1981, 'Problem-centred system therapy of the family', *Journal of Marital and Family Therapy* 7, pp23–31.

Estes C, 1979, *The Ageing Enterprise,* Jossey Bass, San Francisco.

Farran CJ *et al,* 1993, 'Dementia Care Receiver Needs and their Impact on Caregivers', *Clinical Nursing Research* 2(1), pp86–87.

Farrington A, 1995, 'Stress and Nursing', *British Journal of Nursing* 4(10), pp574–578.

Feil N, 1982, *V/F Validation, The Feil Method,* Edward Feil Productions, Cleveland.

Fennell G, Phillipson C & Evers H, 1988, *The Sociology of Old Age,* Open University Press, Milton Keynes.

Finch J and Groves D, 1980, 'Community Care and the Family: a case for equal opportunities?', *Journal of Social Policy* 9(4), pp487–514.

Finch J & Mason J, 1992, *Negotiating Family Responsibilities,* Routledge, London.

Finkelhor D & Pillemer K, 1988, 'The Prevalence of Elder Abuse, A random sample survey', *The Gerontologist* 28(1), pp51–57.

Foner N, 1994, 'Nursing Home Aides: Saints or Monsters?', *The Gerontologist* 34(2), pp245–250.

Gallagher D *et al,* 1989, 'Prevalence of Depression in Family Caregivers', *The Gerontologist* 29(4), pp449–456.

Gilhooley MLM, 1984, 'The impact of caregiving on caregivers, Factors associated with the psychological well being of people supporting a dementing relative in the community', *British Journal of Medical Psychology* 57, pp35–44.

Gilleard C, 1996, 'Family Therapy with Older Clients', Woods RT, (ed), *Handbook of the Clinical Psychology of Ageing,* John Wiley and Sons, Chichester.

Giordano NH & Giordano JA, 1984, 'Elder Abuse: A Review of the Literature', *Social Work* 29(3), pp232–236.

Glendenning F, 1993, 'What is Elder Abuse and Neglect?', Decalmer P & Glendenning F (eds), *The Mistreatment of Elderly People,* Sage, London.

Goffman E, 1961, *Asylums,* Doubleday, Anchor Books, New York.

Goldwasser AN *et al,* 1987, 'Cognitive, Affective and Behavioural Effects of Reminiscence Group Therapy on Demented Elderly', *International Journal of Aging and Human Development* 25, pp209–222.

Goudie F & Stokes G, (1989), 'Understanding Confusion', *Nursing Times* 85(39), pp35–37.

Grafstrom M, Norberg A & Wimblad B, 1993, 'Abuse is in the Eye of the Beholder', *Scandinavian Journal of Social Medicine* 21(4), pp247–255.

Griffiths A, Roberts G & Williams J, 1993, 'Elder Abuse and the Law', Decalmer P & Gendenning F (eds), *The Mistreatment of Elderly People,* Sage, London.

Griffiths A & Roberts G, 1995, *The Law and Elderly People,* Routledge, London.

Gross RD, 1992, *Psychology, The Science of Mind and Behaviour,* Hodder & Stoughton, Sevenoaks.

Hamilton GP, 1989, 'Using a Family Systems Approach to Prevent Elder Abuse', *Journal of Gerontological Nursing* 15(3), pp21–26.

Hansson RO & Carpenter BN, 1994, *Relationships in Old Age: Coping with the Challenge of Transition,* Guilford Press, New York.

Harding N & Palfrey C, 1997, *The Social Construction of Dementia, Confused Professionals?,* Jessica Kingsley, London.

Hockey J, 1989, 'Residential Care and the Maintenance of Social Identity; Negotiating the Transition to Institutional Life', Jeffreys M (ed), *Growing Old in the Twentieth Century,* Routledge, London.

Hockey J & James A, 1994, *Growing Up and Growing Old, Ageing and Dependency in the Life Course,* Sage, London.

Holingbery R, 1999, 'You can't ring the bell!', *Journal of the British Society of Gerontology* 9(1), pp17–19.

Homer A & Gilleard C, 1990, 'Abuse of Elderly People by their Carers', *British Medical Journal* 301, pp1359–1362.

Hooker K et al, 1992, 'Mental and Physical Health of Spouse Caregivers: The Role of Personality', *Psychology and Ageing* 7(3), pp367–375.

Hough M & Mayhew P, 1983, *The British Crime Survey,* Home Office Research Study no 76, HMSO, London.

Itzin C, 1986, 'Ageism Awareness Training, a model for group work', Phillipson C, Bernard M & Strang P (eds), *Dependency and Interdependency in Old Age, Theoretical Perspectives and Policy Alternatives,* Croom Helm, London.

Jarvis C, 1993, 'Family and Friends in Old Age, and the Implications for Informal Support', Working Paper 6, Age Concern Institute of Gerontology.

Jeffreys M & Thane P, 1989, 'Introduction, An Ageing Society and Ageing People', Jeffreys M (ed), *Growing Old in the Twentieth Century,* Routledge, London.

Jerrome D, 1993, 'Intimate Relationships', Bond J & Coleman P (eds), *Ageing in Society: an Introduction to Social Gerontology,* Sage, London.

Johnson J , 1993, 'Does Group Living Work?', Johnson J & Slater R (eds), *Ageing and Later Life,* Sage, London.

Johnson TF, 1991, *Elder Mistreatment: Deciding who is at risk,* Greenwood Press, New York.

Jones DA & Peters TJ, 1992, 'Caring for Elderly Dependents: Effects on the Carers Quality of Life', *Age and Ageing* 21(6), pp421–428.

Jones G, 1992, 'A Communication Model for Dementia' in Jones G & Miesen BML (eds), *Caregiving in Dementia, Research and Applications,* Routledge, London.

Kennedy LW & Silverson RA, 1983, 'Significant Others and Fear of Crime Among The Elderly', *The International Journal of Human Ageing and Development* 20(4), pp241–256.

Kenny M, 1992, 'Punish or we are all Dammed', *Daily Mail,* 11 June, p6.

Kingston P & Penhale B, 1995, 'Social Perspectives on Elder Abuse', Kingston P & Penhale B (eds), *Family Violence and the Caring Professions,* Macmillan, London.

Kitwood T, 1997, *Dementia Reconsidered, The Person Comes First,* Open University Press, Buckingham.

Laing W, 1995, *Laing's Review of Private Health Care, 1995,* Laing and Buisson, London.

Langan J & Means R, 1994, 'Money Management and Elderly People with Dementia', *Elders* 3(3), pp33–42.

Lau E & Kosberg JI, 1979, 'Abuse of the Elderly by Informal Care Providers', *Ageing,* p299–301.

Law Commission, 1991, *Mentally Incapacitated Adults and Decision Making, an Overview,* Consultation Paper 119, HMSO, London.

Lee Treweek G, 1994, 'Bedroom Abuse: The Hidden Work in a Nursing Home', *Generations Review, The Journal of The British Society of Gerontology* 4(2), pp2–4.

Leroux TG & Petrunik M, 1990, 'The construction of elder abuse as a social problem, a Canadian Perspective', *International Journal of Health Services* 20, pp651–663.

Levenson RW, Carstensen LL & Goffman JM, 1993, 'Long Term Marriage: Age Gender and Satisfaction', *Psychology and Ageing* 8(2), pp301–313.

Levine J & Lawlor BA, 1991, 'Family counselling and Legal Issues in Alzheimers Disease', *The Psychiatric Clinics of North America* 14(2), pp385–396.

Maslow AH, 1954, *Motivation and Personality,* Harper Row, New York.

McCreadie C, 1991, *Elder Abuse, An Exploratory Study,* Age Concern Institute of Gerontology, King's College, London.

McCreadie C, 1996, *Elder Abuse: Update on Research,* Age Concern Institute of Gerontology, King's College, London.

McDonald A & Taylor M, 1993, *Elders and the Law,* Pepar Publications, Birmingham.

McDonald A, 1993, 'Elder Abuse and Neglect, the legal framework', *Journal of Elder Abuse and Neglect* 5(2), pp81–96.

MacEwen KE, 1994, 'Refining the Intergenerational Transmission Hypothesis', *Journal of Interpersonal Violence* 9(3), pp350–65.

Meddaugh DI, (1993), 'Covert Elder Abuse in Nursing Homes' *Journal of Elder Abuse and Neglect* 5(3), pp21–37.

Milburn M *et al,* 1995, 'Nursing Care that Patients Value', *British Journal of Nursing* 4(18), pp1094–1098.

National Institute for Social Work, 1988, *Residential Care: A Positive Choice,* HMSO, London.

Neidhardt ER & Allen JA, 1993, *Family Therapy with the Elderly,* Sage, Thousand Oaks.

Nolan M, 1993, 'Carer-Dependent Relationships and the Prevention of Elder Abuse', Decalmer P & Glendenning F (eds), *The Mistreatment of Elderly People,* Sage, London.

Nolan M, 1994, 'Deregulation of Nursing Homes: A Disaster Waiting to Happen?', *British Journal of Nursing* 3(12), p595.

Nolan MR, Grant G & Ellis NC, 1990, 'Stress is in the Eye of the Beholder: Reconceptualising the Measurement of Carer Burden', *Journal of Advanced Nursing* 15, pp544–555.

Norman A, 1980, *Rights and Risks,* Centre for Policy on Ageing, London.

Norman A, 1985, *Triple Jeopardy, Growing Old in a Second Homeland,* Centre for Policy on Ageing, London.

Ogg J & Bennett G, 1992, 'Elder Abuse in Britain', *British Medical Journal* 305, pp 998–999.

Parkinson F, 1993, *Post Trauma Stress,* Sheldon Press, London.

Paveza GJ et al, 1992, 'Severe Family Violence and Alzheimers Disease: Prevalence and Risk Factors', *The Gerontologist* 32(4), pp493–497.

Peace S, Kellaher L & Willcocks D, 1997, *Re-evaluating Residential Care,* Open University Press, Buckingham.

Pearlin LI, Mullan JT, Semple GJ & Skaff MM, 1990, 'Caregiving and the Stress Process: An Overview of Concepts and their Measures', *The Gerontologist* 30(5), pp583–594.

Phillips LR & Rempusheski VF, 1986, 'Caring for the Frail Elderly at Home: Towards a Theoretical Explanation of the Dynamics of Poor Quality Family Care', *Advances in Nursing Science* 8(4), pp62–84.

Phillipson C, 1993a, 'Elder Abuse and Neglect, Social Policy Issues' Working Paper no 1, *Action on Elder Abuse,* Keele University.

Phillipson C, 1993b, 'Abuse of Older People, Sociological Perspectives', Decalmer P & Glendenning F (eds), *The Mistreatment of Elderly People,* Sage, London.

Pietrukowicz ME et al, 1991, 'Using Life Histories to Individualise Nursing Home Staff Attitudes Toward Residents', *The Gerontologist* 31(1), pp102–106.

Pillemer K, 1986, 'Risk factors in elder abuse: Results from a case controlled study', Pillemer K & Wolf R (eds), *Elder Abuse; Conflict in the Family,* Auburn House, Dover.

Pillemer K, 1988, 'Maltreatment of Patients in Nursing Homes: overview and research agenda', *Journal of Health and Social Behaviour* l29(3), pp227–238.

Pillemer K & Finkelhor D, 1988, 'The Prevalence of Elder Abuse, a random sample survey', *The Gerontologist* 28(19), pp51–57.

Pillemer K & Moore DW, 1989b, 'Abuse of Patients in Nursing Homes: Findings from a survey of staff', *The Gerontologist* 29(3), pp314–320.

Pillemer K, 1993, 'Methodological Issues in the Study of Elder Abuse', Working Paper 1, *Action on Elder Abuse,* London.

Pillemer K & Suitor J, 1992, 'Violence and Violent Feelings: What Causes them Among Family Caregivers?', *Journal of Gerontology* 47(4), ppS165–S172.

Poulshock SW & Diemling GT, 1984, 'Caring For Elders in Residence: Issues in the Measurement of Burden', *Journal of Gerontology* 39(2), pp230–239.

Powell-Lawton M, 1981, 'Crime,Victimisation and the Fortitude of the Aged', *Aged Care and Services Review* 2(4), pp20–31.

Pruchno R & Kleban MH, 1993, 'Caring for an Institutionalised Parent, The Role of Coping Strategies', *Psychology and Aging* 8(1), pp18–25.

Qureshi H &Walker A, 1989, *The Caring Relationship; Elderly People and their Families,* Macmillan, London.

Ramsey Klawsnik H, 1991, 'Elder Sexual Abuse: Preliminary Findings', *Journal of Elder Abuse and Neglect* 3(3), pp73–90.

Rankin ED, Haut MW & Keefover RW, 1992, 'Clinical assessment of family caregivers in dementia', *The Gerontologist* 32(6), pp813–821.

Rathbone-McCuan E & Voyles B, 1982, 'Case detection of Abused Elderly Parents', *American Journal of Psychiatry* 139(2), pp189–192.

Raynes N, 1999, 'Older Residents' Participation in Specifying Quality in Nursing and Residential Care Homes', *Generations Review, The Journal of the British Society of Gerontology* 9(2), pp10–12.

Reid WJ & Epstein L, 1972, *Task Centred Casework,* Columbia University, New York.

Riley P, 1989, 'Professional Dilemmas in Elder Abuse', Seminar on Elder Abuse, Association of Welsh Health Authorities, 28th September

Robb B, 1967, *Sans Everything, a Case to Answer,* Thomas Nelson, Sunbury-on-Thames.

Rosenthal CJ et al, 1993, 'Depressive Symptoms in Family Caregivers of Long Stay Patients', *The Gerontologist* 33(2), pp249–257.

Rowe J, Davies K, Barburaj V & Sinha R, 1993, 'F.A.D.E. A.W.A.Y. The Financial Affairs of Dementing Elders, and Who is the Attorney?', *Journal of Elder Abuse and Neglect* 5(2), pp73–79.

Royal College of Nursing, 1994, *An Inspector Calls?,* The Royal College of Nursing, London.

Schaufeli WB & Janczur B, 1994, 'Burnout Among Nurses, A Polish Dutch Comparison', *Journal of Cross Cultural Psychology* 25(1), pp95–113.

Schulz R & Williamson GM, 1991, 'A 2 Year Longitudinal Study of Depression among Alzheimers Caregivers', *Psychology and Aging* 6(4), pp569–578.

Seaton M, 1994, 'A Duty to Care, Control and Restraint', *Elders* 3(4), pp5–19.

Seligman MEP, 1975, *Helplessness: On Depression, Development and Death,* Freeman Press, San Francisco.

Sheilds CG, 1992, 'Family interaction and caregivers of Alzheimers disease patients, correlations of depression', *Family Process* 31, pp19–33.

Sidell M, 1995, *Health in Old Age, Myth, Mystery and Management,* Open University Press, Buckingham.

Silverstein M & Bengston VL, 1991, 'Do close parent–child relations reduce the mortality risk of older parents?', *Journal of Health and Social Behaviour* 32, pp382–395.

Skaff MM & Pearlin LI, 1992, 'Caregiving: Role Enlightenment and the Loss of Self', *The Gerontologist* 32(5),pp656–664.

Stannard CI, 1973, 'Old Fools and Dirty Work: The Social Conditions for Patient Abuse in a Nursing Home', *Social Problems* 20, pp329–342.

Steinmetz SK, 1988, *Duty Bound, Elder Abuse and Family Care,* Sage, Thousand Oaks.

Stetz KM & Hanson WK, 1992, 'Alterations in Perceptions of Caregiving Demands in Advanced Cancer, During and After the Experience', *The Hospice Journal* 8(3), pp21–34.

Stevenson O, 1988, *Age and Vulnerability, a guide to better care,* Edward Arnold, London.

Stokes G & Goudie F, 1990, *Working With Dementia,* Winslow Press, Bicester.

Southwark Social Services, 1987, *Report of the Inquiry into Nye Bevan Lodge,* Southwark Social Services, London.

Thomas PD *et al*, 1985, 'Effects of social support on stress related changes in cholesterol level, uric acid and immune function in an elderly sample', *American Journal of Psychiatry* 142, pp735–737.

Townsend P, 1986, 'Ageism and Social Policy' in Phillipson C & Walker A (eds), *Ageing and Social Policy*, Gower Press, Aldershot.

Townsend P, 1962, *The Last Refuge,* Routledge & Kegan Paul, London.

Twigg J & Atkin K, 1994, *Carers Perceived, Policy and Practice in Informal Care,* Open University Press, Buckingham.

United Kingdom Central Council for Nursing Midwifery and Health Visiting, 1994, *Professional Conduct-Occasional Report on Standards of Nursing in Nursing Homes,* UKCC, London.

Victor C, 1987, *Old Age in Modern Society,* Chapman & Hall, London.

Victor C, 1991, *Health and Health Care in Later Life*, Open University Press, Buckingham.

Wagner G, 1988, *Residential Care, a Positive Choice,* Report of the Independent Review of Residential Care, HMSO, London.

Wallhagen MI, 1992, 'Caregiving Demands: Their Difficulty and Effects on the Wellbeing of Elderly Caregivers', *Scholarly Enquiry For Nursing Practice: An International Journal* 6(2), pp111–127.

Whatmore K & Mira-Smith C, 1991, 'Elder Care in the Nineties', *National Carers Survey Research Team,* London.

Willcocks D, Peace S & Kellaher L, 1987, *Private Lives In Public Places,* Tavistock, London.

Williams J, 1992, 'Legal Capacity and Older People', Griffiths A *et al* (eds), *Sharpening the Instrument, the Law and Older People,* Base Publication.

Wilson G, 1990, 'Elder Abuse: a hidden horror', *Critical Public Health* 2, pp32–38.

Wolf RS, 1994, 'Elder Abuse, A Family Tragedy', *Ageing International* March, pp60–64.

Wolf R & Pillemer K, 1989, *Helping Elderly Victims, The Reality of Elder Abuse,* Columbia University Press, New York.

Wright S, 1992, 'Quality Assurance in Department of Health' (ed), *Long Term Care for Elderly People; Purchasing, Providing and Quality,* HMSO, London.

Yawney BA & Slover DL, 1973, 'Relocation of the Elderly', *Social Work* 18, pp86–89.